C-2950  CAREER EXAMINATION SERIES

*This is your*
*PASSBOOK for...*

# Public Information Officer

*Test Preparation Study Guide*
*Questions & Answers*

NLC®

**NATIONAL LEARNING CORPORATION**®

# COPYRIGHT NOTICE

This book is SOLELY intended for, is sold ONLY to, and its use is RESTRICTED to individual, bona fide applicants or candidates who qualify by virtue of having seriously filed applications for appropriate license, certificate, professional and/or promotional advancement, higher school matriculation, scholarship, or other legitimate requirements of education and/or governmental authorities.

This book is NOT intended for use, class instruction, tutoring, training, duplication, copying, reprinting, excerption, or adaptation, etc., by:

1) Other publishers
2) Proprietors and/or Instructors of "Coaching" and/or Preparatory Courses
3) Personnel and/or Training Divisions of commercial, industrial, and governmental organizations
4) Schools, colleges, or universities and/or their departments and staffs, including teachers and other personnel
5) Testing Agencies or Bureaus
6) Study groups which seek by the purchase of a single volume to copy and/or duplicate and/or adapt this material for use by the group as a whole without having purchased individual volumes for each of the members of the group
7) Et al.

Such persons would be in violation of appropriate Federal and State statutes.

PROVISION OF LICENSING AGREEMENTS – Recognized educational, commercial, industrial, and governmental institutions and organizations, and others legitimately engaged in educational pursuits, including training, testing, and measurement activities, may address request for a licensing agreement to the copyright owners, who will determine whether, and under what conditions, including fees and charges, the materials in this book may be used them. In other words, a licensing facility exists for the legitimate use of the material in this book on other than an individual basis. However, it is asseverated and affirmed here that the material in this book CANNOT be used without the receipt of the express permission of such a licensing agreement from the Publishers. Inquiries re licensing should be addressed to the company, attention rights and permissions department.

All rights reserved, including the right of reproduction in whole or in part, in any form or by any means, electronic or mechanical, including photocopying, recording, or by any information storage and retrieval system, without permission in writing from the Publisher.

Copyright © 2025 by
## National Learning Corporation

212 Michael Drive, Syosset, NY 11791
(516) 921-8888 • www.passbooks.com
E-mail: info@passbooks.com

# PASSBOOK® SERIES

THE *PASSBOOK® SERIES* has been created to prepare applicants and candidates for the ultimate academic battlefield – the examination room.

At some time in our lives, each and every one of us may be required to take an examination – for validation, matriculation, admission, qualification, registration, certification, or licensure.

Based on the assumption that every applicant or candidate has met the basic formal educational standards, has taken the required number of courses, and read the necessary texts, the *PASSBOOK® SERIES* furnishes the one special preparation which may assure passing with confidence, instead of failing with insecurity. Examination questions – together with answers – are furnished as the basic vehicle for study so that the mysteries of the examination and its compounding difficulties may be eliminated or diminished by a sure method.

This book is meant to help you pass your examination provided that you qualify and are serious in your objective.

The entire field is reviewed through the huge store of content information which is succinctly presented through a provocative and challenging approach – the question-and-answer method.

A climate of success is established by furnishing the correct answers at the end of each test.

You soon learn to recognize types of questions, forms of questions, and patterns of questioning. You may even begin to anticipate expected outcomes.

You perceive that many questions are repeated or adapted so that you can gain acute insights, which may enable you to score many sure points.

You learn how to confront new questions, or types of questions, and to attack them confidently and work out the correct answers.

You note objectives and emphases, and recognize pitfalls and dangers, so that you may make positive educational adjustments.

Moreover, you are kept fully informed in relation to new concepts, methods, practices, and directions in the field.

You discover that you are actually taking the examination all the time: you are preparing for the examination by "taking" an examination, not by reading extraneous and/or supererogatory textbooks.

In short, this PASSBOOK®, used directedly, should be an important factor in helping you to pass your test.

# PUBLIC INFORMATION OFFICER

DUTIES:
  Develops, organizes, and directs a comprehensive public information program; performs related duties as required.
  Under direction, plans, directs, and performs work involved in the collection, preparation, and dissemination of information regarding the plans, goals, programs, and achievements of the agency or jurisdiction through newspaper, radio, television, flyers, periodicals, and other media; furnishes advice and consultation to management concerning the information needs of the public; does other related duties.

EXAMPLES OF WORK:
- Determines the objectives of the informational program and the methods by which they will be put into effect in terms of available resources and agency priorities; plans media coverage and methods to present the desired information to the public.
- Plans public information programs and disseminates information to inform the public or affected groups about the work of the agency.
- Writes, edits, or oversees the writing and editing of copy; reviews and evaluates for policy and content; styles informational and promotional materials such as press releases, publications, radio and television programs, and photographs; assesses the value and effectiveness of written material in achieving agency's information and program objectives.
- Incorporates the basic philosophy of management in speeches and in other written or printed material; interprets facts as presented.
- May arrange and direct press conferences, radio, or television interviews of management officials.
- May conduct information programs to inform employees of activities, agency performance, and of applicable administrative decisions.
- Establishes and maintains liaison and cooperative working relationships with media representatives and with interested public, private, and voluntary groups to ensure understanding of the agency's programs and to create and maintain a favorable public image.
- May supervise technical assistants and other employees; may be responsible for effectively recommending the hiring, firing, promoting, demoting, and/or disciplining of employees.
- Selects appropriate subject matter; collects data relating to issues from varied sources, draws reasonable unbiased conclusions, and utilizes facts pertinent to specific cases to prepare clear, concise, and informative articles and news releases for publication.
- May arrange for, and/or conduct meeting and public contact programs to familiarize residents, community groups, business concerns, nonprofit organizations, and other government agencies with the activities of the agency; may select speakers for public meetings.
- May conduct or oversee public surveys and other information gathering activities designed to identify public or consumer interests, attitudes, and habits.

SUBJECT OF EXAMINATION:

The written test is designed to evaluate knowledge, skills and /or abilities in the following areas:

1. **Directing a public information program or project** - These questions test for a knowledge of the standards and practices used in preparing information for the public or for the print, electronic, or broadcast media. Questions may cover such topics as conducting research, developing content, selecting methods of communication, and coordinating the production of the final product.
2. **Educating and interacting with the public** - These questions test for the ability to communicate with others in a manner consistent with good public relations practices. Questions will cover such concepts as interviewing or gathering information from others; participating in meetings or work groups; and presenting information to citizens, community organizations, staff and the media.
3. **Grammar, usage, punctuation, and editing** - These questions test for the ability to prepare letters, reports, and other documents. Some questions test for a knowledge of grammar, usage, punctuation, and sentence structure. Others test for the ability to edit sentences to produce correct, clear, concise copy.
4. **Preparing public information materials** - These questions test for a knowledge of professional standards and practices used to produce public information materials for print, electronic, or broadcast media. Questions may cover such topics as developing content, selecting media, and coordinating the posting or distribution of information.
5. **Preparing written material** - These questions test for the ability to present information clearly and accurately, and to organize paragraphs logically and comprehensibly. For some questions, you will be given information in two or three sentences followed by four restatements of the information. You must then choose the best version. For other questions, you will be given paragraphs with their sentences out of order. You must then choose, from four suggestions, the best order for the sentences.
6. **Supervision** - These questions test for knowledge of the principles and practices employed in planning, organizing, and controlling the activities of a work unit toward predetermined objectives. The concepts covered, usually in a situational question format, include such topics as assigning and reviewing work; evaluating performance; maintaining work standards; motivating and developing subordinates; implementing procedural change; increasing efficiency; and dealing with problems of absenteeism, morale, and discipline.

# HOW TO TAKE A TEST

I. YOU MUST PASS AN EXAMINATION

A. *WHAT EVERY CANDIDATE SHOULD KNOW*

Examination applicants often ask us for help in preparing for the written test. What can I study in advance? What kinds of questions will be asked? How will the test be given? How will the papers be graded?

As an applicant for a civil service examination, you may be wondering about some of these things. Our purpose here is to suggest effective methods of advance study and to describe civil service examinations.

Your chances for success on this examination can be increased if you know how to prepare. Those "pre-examination jitters" can be reduced if you know what to expect. You can even experience an adventure in good citizenship if you know why civil service exams are given.

B. *WHY ARE CIVIL SERVICE EXAMINATIONS GIVEN?*

Civil service examinations are important to you in two ways. As a citizen, you want public jobs filled by employees who know how to do their work. As a job seeker, you want a fair chance to compete for that job on an equal footing with other candidates. The best-known means of accomplishing this two-fold goal is the competitive examination.

Exams are widely publicized throughout the nation. They may be administered for jobs in federal, state, city, municipal, town or village governments or agencies.

Any citizen may apply, with some limitations, such as the age or residence of applicants. Your experience and education may be reviewed to see whether you meet the requirements for the particular examination. When these requirements exist, they are reasonable and applied consistently to all applicants. Thus, a competitive examination may cause you some uneasiness now, but it is your privilege and safeguard.

C. *HOW ARE CIVIL SERVICE EXAMS DEVELOPED?*

Examinations are carefully written by trained technicians who are specialists in the field known as "psychological measurement," in consultation with recognized authorities in the field of work that the test will cover. These experts recommend the subject matter areas or skills to be tested; only those knowledges or skills important to your success on the job are included. The most reliable books and source materials available are used as references. Together, the experts and technicians judge the difficulty level of the questions.

Test technicians know how to phrase questions so that the problem is clearly stated. Their ethics do not permit "trick" or "catch" questions. Questions may have been tried out on sample groups, or subjected to statistical analysis, to determine their usefulness.

Written tests are often used in combination with performance tests, ratings of training and experience, and oral interviews. All of these measures combine to form the best-known means of finding the right person for the right job.

## II. HOW TO PASS THE WRITTEN TEST

### A. NATURE OF THE EXAMINATION

To prepare intelligently for civil service examinations, you should know how they differ from school examinations you have taken. In school you were assigned certain definite pages to read or subjects to cover. The examination questions were quite detailed and usually emphasized memory. Civil service exams, on the other hand, try to discover your present ability to perform the duties of a position, plus your potentiality to learn these duties. In other words, a civil service exam attempts to predict how successful you will be. Questions cover such a broad area that they cannot be as minute and detailed as school exam questions.

In the public service similar kinds of work, or positions, are grouped together in one "class." This process is known as *position-classification*. All the positions in a class are paid according to the salary range for that class. One class title covers all of these positions, and they are all tested by the same examination.

### B. FOUR BASIC STEPS

#### 1) Study the announcement

How, then, can you know what subjects to study? Our best answer is: "Learn as much as possible about the class of positions for which you've applied." The exam will test the knowledge, skills and abilities needed to do the work.

Your most valuable source of information about the position you want is the official exam announcement. This announcement lists the training and experience qualifications. Check these standards and apply only if you come reasonably close to meeting them.

The brief description of the position in the examination announcement offers some clues to the subjects which will be tested. Think about the job itself. Review the duties in your mind. Can you perform them, or are there some in which you are rusty? Fill in the blank spots in your preparation.

Many jurisdictions preview the written test in the exam announcement by including a section called "Knowledge and Abilities Required," "Scope of the Examination," or some similar heading. Here you will find out specifically what fields will be tested.

#### 2) Review your own background

Once you learn in general what the position is all about, and what you need to know to do the work, ask yourself which subjects you already know fairly well and which need improvement. You may wonder whether to concentrate on improving your strong areas or on building some background in your fields of weakness. When the announcement has specified "some knowledge" or "considerable knowledge," or has used adjectives like "beginning principles of..." or "advanced ... methods," you can get a clue as to the number and difficulty of questions to be asked in any given field. More questions, and hence broader coverage, would be included for those subjects which are more important in the work. Now weigh your strengths and weaknesses against the job requirements and prepare accordingly.

#### 3) Determine the level of the position

Another way to tell how intensively you should prepare is to understand the level of the job for which you are applying. Is it the entering level? In other words, is this the position in which beginners in a field of work are hired? Or is it an intermediate or advanced level? Sometimes this is indicated by such words as "Junior" or "Senior" in the class title. Other jurisdictions use Roman numerals to designate the level – Clerk I, Clerk II, for example. The word "Supervisor" sometimes appears in the title. If the level is not indicated by the title, check the description of duties. Will you be working under very close supervision, or will you have responsibility for independent decisions in this work?

### 4) Choose appropriate study materials

Now that you know the subjects to be examined and the relative amount of each subject to be covered, you can choose suitable study materials. For beginning level jobs, or even advanced ones, if you have a pronounced weakness in some aspect of your training, read a modern, standard textbook in that field. Be sure it is up to date and has general coverage. Such books are normally available at your library, and the librarian will be glad to help you locate one. For entry-level positions, questions of appropriate difficulty are chosen – neither highly advanced questions, nor those too simple. Such questions require careful thought but not advanced training.

If the position for which you are applying is technical or advanced, you will read more advanced, specialized material. If you are already familiar with the basic principles of your field, elementary textbooks would waste your time. Concentrate on advanced textbooks and technical periodicals. Think through the concepts and review difficult problems in your field.

These are all general sources. You can get more ideas on your own initiative, following these leads. For example, training manuals and publications of the government agency which employs workers in your field can be useful, particularly for technical and professional positions. A letter or visit to the government department involved may result in more specific study suggestions, and certainly will provide you with a more definite idea of the exact nature of the position you are seeking.

## III. KINDS OF TESTS

Tests are used for purposes other than measuring knowledge and ability to perform specified duties. For some positions, it is equally important to test ability to make adjustments to new situations or to profit from training. In others, basic mental abilities not dependent on information are essential. Questions which test these things may not appear as pertinent to the duties of the position as those which test for knowledge and information. Yet they are often highly important parts of a fair examination. For very general questions, it is almost impossible to help you direct your study efforts. What we can do is to point out some of the more common of these general abilities needed in public service positions and describe some typical questions.

1) General information

Broad, general information has been found useful for predicting job success in some kinds of work. This is tested in a variety of ways, from vocabulary lists to questions about current events. Basic background in some field of work, such as sociology or economics, may be sampled in a group of questions. Often these are principles which have become familiar to most persons through exposure rather than through formal training. It is difficult to advise you how to study for these questions; being alert to the world around you is our best suggestion.

2) Verbal ability

An example of an ability needed in many positions is verbal or language ability. Verbal ability is, in brief, the ability to use and understand words. Vocabulary and grammar tests are typical measures of this ability. Reading comprehension or paragraph interpretation questions are common in many kinds of civil service tests. You are given a paragraph of written material and asked to find its central meaning.

3) Numerical ability

Number skills can be tested by the familiar arithmetic problem, by checking paired lists of numbers to see which are alike and which are different, or by interpreting charts and graphs. In the latter test, a graph may be printed in the test booklet which you are asked to use as the basis for answering questions.

4) Observation

A popular test for law-enforcement positions is the observation test. A picture is shown to you for several minutes, then taken away. Questions about the picture test your ability to observe both details and larger elements.

5) Following directions

In many positions in the public service, the employee must be able to carry out written instructions dependably and accurately. You may be given a chart with several columns, each column listing a variety of information. The questions require you to carry out directions involving the information given in the chart.

6) Skills and aptitudes

Performance tests effectively measure some manual skills and aptitudes. When the skill is one in which you are trained, such as typing or shorthand, you can practice. These tests are often very much like those given in business school or high school courses. For many of the other skills and aptitudes, however, no short-time preparation can be made. Skills and abilities natural to you or that you have developed throughout your lifetime are being tested.

Many of the general questions just described provide all the data needed to answer the questions and ask you to use your reasoning ability to find the answers. Your best preparation for these tests, as well as for tests of facts and ideas, is to be at your physical and mental best. You, no doubt, have your own methods of getting into an exam-taking mood and keeping "in shape." The next section lists some ideas on this subject.

IV. KINDS OF QUESTIONS

Only rarely is the "essay" question, which you answer in narrative form, used in civil service tests. Civil service tests are usually of the short-answer type. Full instructions for answering these questions will be given to you at the examination. But in case this is your first experience with short-answer questions and separate answer sheets, here is what you need to know:

**1) Multiple-choice Questions**

Most popular of the short-answer questions is the "multiple choice" or "best answer" question. It can be used, for example, to test for factual knowledge, ability to solve problems or judgment in meeting situations found at work.

A multiple-choice question is normally one of three types—
- It can begin with an incomplete statement followed by several possible endings. You are to find the one ending which *best* completes the statement, although some of the others may not be entirely wrong.
- It can also be a complete statement in the form of a question which is answered by choosing one of the statements listed.

- It can be in the form of a problem – again you select the best answer.

Here is an example of a multiple-choice question with a discussion which should give you some clues as to the method for choosing the right answer:

When an employee has a complaint about his assignment, the action which will *best* help him overcome his difficulty is to
- A. discuss his difficulty with his coworkers
- B. take the problem to the head of the organization
- C. take the problem to the person who gave him the assignment
- D. say nothing to anyone about his complaint

In answering this question, you should study each of the choices to find which is best. Consider choice "A" – Certainly an employee may discuss his complaint with fellow employees, but no change or improvement can result, and the complaint remains unresolved. Choice "B" is a poor choice since the head of the organization probably does not know what assignment you have been given, and taking your problem to him is known as "going over the head" of the supervisor. The supervisor, or person who made the assignment, is the person who can clarify it or correct any injustice. Choice "C" is, therefore, correct. To say nothing, as in choice "D," is unwise. Supervisors have and interest in knowing the problems employees are facing, and the employee is seeking a solution to his problem.

## 2) True/False Questions

The "true/false" or "right/wrong" form of question is sometimes used. Here a complete statement is given. Your job is to decide whether the statement is right or wrong.

SAMPLE: A roaming cell-phone call to a nearby city costs less than a non-roaming call to a distant city.

This statement is wrong, or false, since roaming calls are more expensive.

This is not a complete list of all possible question forms, although most of the others are variations of these common types. You will always get complete directions for answering questions. Be sure you understand *how* to mark your answers – ask questions until you do.

## V. RECORDING YOUR ANSWERS

Computer terminals are used more and more today for many different kinds of exams.
For an examination with very few applicants, you may be told to record your answers in the test booklet itself. Separate answer sheets are much more common. If this separate answer sheet is to be scored by machine – and this is often the case – it is highly important that you mark your answers correctly in order to get credit.
An electronic scoring machine is often used in civil service offices because of the speed with which papers can be scored. Machine-scored answer sheets must be marked with a pencil, which will be given to you. This pencil has a high graphite content which responds to the electronic scoring machine. As a matter of fact, stray dots may register as answers, so do not let your pencil rest on the answer sheet while you are pondering the correct answer. Also, if your pencil lead breaks or is otherwise defective, ask for another.

Since the answer sheet will be dropped in a slot in the scoring machine, be careful not to bend the corners or get the paper crumpled.

The answer sheet normally has five vertical columns of numbers, with 30 numbers to a column. These numbers correspond to the question numbers in your test booklet. After each number, going across the page are four or five pairs of dotted lines. These short dotted lines have small letters or numbers above them. The first two pairs may also have a "T" or "F" above the letters. This indicates that the first two pairs only are to be used if the questions are of the true-false type. If the questions are multiple choice, disregard the "T" and "F" and pay attention only to the small letters or numbers.

Answer your questions in the manner of the sample that follows:

32. The largest city in the United States is
    A. Washington, D.C.
    B. New York City
    C. Chicago
    D. Detroit
    E. San Francisco

1) Choose the answer you think is best. (New York City is the largest, so "B" is correct.)
2) Find the row of dotted lines numbered the same as the question you are answering. (Find row number 32)
3) Find the pair of dotted lines corresponding to the answer. (Find the pair of lines under the mark "B.")
4) Make a solid black mark between the dotted lines.

## VI. BEFORE THE TEST

Common sense will help you find procedures to follow to get ready for an examination. Too many of us, however, overlook these sensible measures. Indeed, nervousness and fatigue have been found to be the most serious reasons why applicants fail to do their best on civil service tests. Here is a list of reminders:

- Begin your preparation early – Don't wait until the last minute to go scurrying around for books and materials or to find out what the position is all about.
- Prepare continuously – An hour a night for a week is better than an all-night cram session. This has been definitely established. What is more, a night a week for a month will return better dividends than crowding your study into a shorter period of time.
- Locate the place of the exam – You have been sent a notice telling you when and where to report for the examination. If the location is in a different town or otherwise unfamiliar to you, it would be well to inquire the best route and learn something about the building.
- Relax the night before the test – Allow your mind to rest. Do not study at all that night. Plan some mild recreation or diversion; then go to bed early and get a good night's sleep.
- Get up early enough to make a leisurely trip to the place for the test – This way unforeseen events, traffic snarls, unfamiliar buildings, etc. will not upset you.
- Dress comfortably – A written test is not a fashion show. You will be known by number and not by name, so wear something comfortable.

- Leave excess paraphernalia at home – Shopping bags and odd bundles will get in your way. You need bring only the items mentioned in the official notice you received; usually everything you need is provided. Do not bring reference books to the exam. They will only confuse those last minutes and be taken away from you when in the test room.
- Arrive somewhat ahead of time – If because of transportation schedules you must get there very early, bring a newspaper or magazine to take your mind off yourself while waiting.
- Locate the examination room – When you have found the proper room, you will be directed to the seat or part of the room where you will sit. Sometimes you are given a sheet of instructions to read while you are waiting. Do not fill out any forms until you are told to do so; just read them and be prepared.
- Relax and prepare to listen to the instructions
- If you have any physical problem that may keep you from doing your best, be sure to tell the test administrator. If you are sick or in poor health, you really cannot do your best on the exam. You can come back and take the test some other time.

## VII. AT THE TEST

The day of the test is here and you have the test booklet in your hand. The temptation to get going is very strong. Caution! There is more to success than knowing the right answers. You must know how to identify your papers and understand variations in the type of short-answer question used in this particular examination. Follow these suggestions for maximum results from your efforts:

### 1) Cooperate with the monitor

The test administrator has a duty to create a situation in which you can be as much at ease as possible. He will give instructions, tell you when to begin, check to see that you are marking your answer sheet correctly, and so on. He is not there to guard you, although he will see that your competitors do not take unfair advantage. He wants to help you do your best.

### 2) Listen to all instructions

Don't jump the gun! Wait until you understand all directions. In most civil service tests you get more time than you need to answer the questions. So don't be in a hurry. Read each word of instructions until you clearly understand the meaning. Study the examples, listen to all announcements and follow directions. Ask questions if you do not understand what to do.

### 3) Identify your papers

Civil service exams are usually identified by number only. You will be assigned a number; you must not put your name on your test papers. Be sure to copy your number correctly. Since more than one exam may be given, copy your exact examination title.

### 4) Plan your time

Unless you are told that a test is a "speed" or "rate of work" test, speed itself is usually not important. Time enough to answer all the questions will be provided, but this does not mean that you have all day. An overall time limit has been set. Divide the total time (in minutes) by the number of questions to determine the approximate time you have for each question.

### 5) Do not linger over difficult questions

If you come across a difficult question, mark it with a paper clip (useful to have along) and come back to it when you have been through the booklet. One caution if you do this – be sure to skip a number on your answer sheet as well. Check often to be sure that you have not lost your place and that you are marking in the row numbered the same as the question you are answering.

### 6) Read the questions

Be sure you know what the question asks! Many capable people are unsuccessful because they failed to *read* the questions correctly.

### 7) Answer all questions

Unless you have been instructed that a penalty will be deducted for incorrect answers, it is better to guess than to omit a question.

### 8) Speed tests

It is often better NOT to guess on speed tests. It has been found that on timed tests people are tempted to spend the last few seconds before time is called in marking answers at random – without even reading them – in the hope of picking up a few extra points. To discourage this practice, the instructions may warn you that your score will be "corrected" for guessing. That is, a penalty will be applied. The incorrect answers will be deducted from the correct ones, or some other penalty formula will be used.

### 9) Review your answers

If you finish before time is called, go back to the questions you guessed or omitted to give them further thought. Review other answers if you have time.

### 10) Return your test materials

If you are ready to leave before others have finished or time is called, take ALL your materials to the monitor and leave quietly. Never take any test material with you. The monitor can discover whose papers are not complete, and taking a test booklet may be grounds for disqualification.

## VIII. EXAMINATION TECHNIQUES

1) Read the general instructions carefully. These are usually printed on the first page of the exam booklet. As a rule, these instructions refer to the timing of the examination; the fact that you should not start work until the signal and must stop work at a signal, etc. If there are any *special* instructions, such as a choice of questions to be answered, make sure that you note this instruction carefully.

2) When you are ready to start work on the examination, that is as soon as the signal has been given, read the instructions to each question booklet, underline any key words or phrases, such as *least, best, outline, describe* and the like. In this way you will tend to answer as requested rather than discover on reviewing your paper that you *listed without describing*, that you selected the *worst* choice rather than the *best* choice, etc.

3) If the examination is of the objective or multiple-choice type – that is, each question will also give a series of possible answers: A, B, C or D, and you are called upon to select the best answer and write the letter next to that answer on your answer paper – it is advisable to start answering each question in turn. There may be anywhere from 50 to 100 such questions in the three or four hours allotted and you can see how much time would be taken if you read through all the questions before beginning to answer any. Furthermore, if you come across a question or group of questions which you know would be difficult to answer, it would undoubtedly affect your handling of all the other questions.

4) If the examination is of the essay type and contains but a few questions, it is a moot point as to whether you should read all the questions before starting to answer any one. Of course, if you are given a choice – say five out of seven and the like – then it is essential to read all the questions so you can eliminate the two that are most difficult. If, however, you are asked to answer all the questions, there may be danger in trying to answer the easiest one first because you may find that you will spend too much time on it. The best technique is to answer the first question, then proceed to the second, etc.

5) Time your answers. Before the exam begins, write down the time it started, then add the time allowed for the examination and write down the time it must be completed, then divide the time available somewhat as follows:
   - If 3-1/2 hours are allowed, that would be 210 minutes. If you have 80 objective-type questions, that would be an average of 2-1/2 minutes per question. Allow yourself no more than 2 minutes per question, or a total of 160 minutes, which will permit about 50 minutes to review.
   - If for the time allotment of 210 minutes there are 7 essay questions to answer, that would average about 30 minutes a question. Give yourself only 25 minutes per question so that you have about 35 minutes to review.

6) The most important instruction is to *read each question* and make sure you know what is wanted. The second most important instruction is to *time yourself properly* so that you answer every question. The third most important instruction is to *answer every question*. Guess if you have to but include something for each question. Remember that you will receive no credit for a blank and will probably receive some credit if you write something in answer to an essay question. If you guess a letter – say "B" for a multiple-choice question – you may have guessed right. If you leave a blank as an answer to a multiple-choice question, the examiners may respect your feelings but it will not add a point to your score. Some exams may penalize you for wrong answers, so in such cases *only*, you may not want to guess unless you have some basis for your answer.

7) Suggestions
   a. Objective-type questions
      1. Examine the question booklet for proper sequence of pages and questions
      2. Read all instructions carefully
      3. Skip any question which seems too difficult; return to it after all other questions have been answered
      4. Apportion your time properly; do not spend too much time on any single question or group of questions

5. Note and underline key words – *all, most, fewest, least, best, worst, same, opposite,* etc.
6. Pay particular attention to negatives
7. Note unusual option, e.g., unduly long, short, complex, different or similar in content to the body of the question
8. Observe the use of "hedging" words – *probably, may, most likely,* etc.
9. Make sure that your answer is put next to the same number as the question
10. Do not second-guess unless you have good reason to believe the second answer is definitely more correct
11. Cross out original answer if you decide another answer is more accurate; do not erase until you are ready to hand your paper in
12. Answer all questions; guess unless instructed otherwise
13. Leave time for review

   b. Essay questions
      1. Read each question carefully
      2. Determine exactly what is wanted. Underline key words or phrases.
      3. Decide on outline or paragraph answer
      4. Include many different points and elements unless asked to develop any one or two points or elements
      5. Show impartiality by giving pros and cons unless directed to select one side only
      6. Make and write down any assumptions you find necessary to answer the questions
      7. Watch your English, grammar, punctuation and choice of words
      8. Time your answers; don't crowd material

8) Answering the essay question

Most essay questions can be answered by framing the specific response around several key words or ideas. Here are a few such key words or ideas:

M's: manpower, materials, methods, money, management
P's: purpose, program, policy, plan, procedure, practice, problems, pitfalls, personnel, public relations

   a. Six basic steps in handling problems:
      1. Preliminary plan and background development
      2. Collect information, data and facts
      3. Analyze and interpret information, data and facts
      4. Analyze and develop solutions as well as make recommendations
      5. Prepare report and sell recommendations
      6. Install recommendations and follow up effectiveness

   b. Pitfalls to avoid
      1. *Taking things for granted* – A statement of the situation does not necessarily imply that each of the elements is necessarily true; for example, a complaint may be invalid and biased so that all that can be taken for granted is that a complaint has been registered

2. *Considering only one side of a situation* – Wherever possible, indicate several alternatives and then point out the reasons you selected the best one
3. *Failing to indicate follow up* – Whenever your answer indicates action on your part, make certain that you will take proper follow-up action to see how successful your recommendations, procedures or actions turn out to be
4. *Taking too long in answering any single question* – Remember to time your answers properly

## IX. AFTER THE TEST

Scoring procedures differ in detail among civil service jurisdictions although the general principles are the same. Whether the papers are hand-scored or graded by machine we have described, they are nearly always graded by number. That is, the person who marks the paper knows only the number – never the name – of the applicant. Not until all the papers have been graded will they be matched with names. If other tests, such as training and experience or oral interview ratings have been given, scores will be combined. Different parts of the examination usually have different weights. For example, the written test might count 60 percent of the final grade, and a rating of training and experience 40 percent. In many jurisdictions, veterans will have a certain number of points added to their grades.

After the final grade has been determined, the names are placed in grade order and an eligible list is established. There are various methods for resolving ties between those who get the same final grade – probably the most common is to place first the name of the person whose application was received first. Job offers are made from the eligible list in the order the names appear on it. You will be notified of your grade and your rank as soon as all these computations have been made. This will be done as rapidly as possible.

People who are found to meet the requirements in the announcement are called "eligibles." Their names are put on a list of eligible candidates. An eligible's chances of getting a job depend on how high he stands on this list and how fast agencies are filling jobs from the list.

When a job is to be filled from a list of eligibles, the agency asks for the names of people on the list of eligibles for that job. When the civil service commission receives this request, it sends to the agency the names of the three people highest on this list. Or, if the job to be filled has specialized requirements, the office sends the agency the names of the top three persons who meet these requirements from the general list.

The appointing officer makes a choice from among the three people whose names were sent to him. If the selected person accepts the appointment, the names of the others are put back on the list to be considered for future openings.

That is the rule in hiring from all kinds of eligible lists, whether they are for typist, carpenter, chemist, or something else. For every vacancy, the appointing officer has his choice of any one of the top three eligibles on the list. This explains why the person whose name is on top of the list sometimes does not get an appointment when some of the persons lower on the list do. If the appointing officer chooses the second or third eligible, the No. 1 eligible does not get a job at once, but stays on the list until he is appointed or the list is terminated.

# X. HOW TO PASS THE INTERVIEW TEST

The examination for which you applied requires an oral interview test. You have already taken the written test and you are now being called for the interview test – the final part of the formal examination.

You may think that it is not possible to prepare for an interview test and that there are no procedures to follow during an interview. Our purpose is to point out some things you can do in advance that will help you and some good rules to follow and pitfalls to avoid while you are being interviewed.

*What is an interview supposed to test?*

The written examination is designed to test the technical knowledge and competence of the candidate; the oral is designed to evaluate intangible qualities, not readily measured otherwise, and to establish a list showing the relative fitness of each candidate – as measured against his competitors – for the position sought. Scoring is not on the basis of "right" and "wrong," but on a sliding scale of values ranging from "not passable" to "outstanding." As a matter of fact, it is possible to achieve a relatively low score without a single "incorrect" answer because of evident weakness in the qualities being measured.

Occasionally, an examination may consist entirely of an oral test – either an individual or a group oral. In such cases, information is sought concerning the technical knowledges and abilities of the candidate, since there has been no written examination for this purpose. More commonly, however, an oral test is used to supplement a written examination.

*Who conducts interviews?*

The composition of oral boards varies among different jurisdictions. In nearly all, a representative of the personnel department serves as chairman. One of the members of the board may be a representative of the department in which the candidate would work. In some cases, "outside experts" are used, and, frequently, a businessman or some other representative of the general public is asked to serve. Labor and management or other special groups may be represented. The aim is to secure the services of experts in the appropriate field.

However the board is composed, it is a good idea (and not at all improper or unethical) to ascertain in advance of the interview who the members are and what groups they represent. When you are introduced to them, you will have some idea of their backgrounds and interests, and at least you will not stutter and stammer over their names.

*What should be done before the interview?*

While knowledge about the board members is useful and takes some of the surprise element out of the interview, there is other preparation which is more substantive. It *is* possible to prepare for an oral interview – in several ways:

### 1) Keep a copy of your application and review it carefully before the interview

This may be the only document before the oral board, and the starting point of the interview. Know what education and experience you have listed there, and the sequence and dates of all of it. Sometimes the board will ask you to review the highlights of your experience for them; you should not have to hem and haw doing it.

### 2) Study the class specification and the examination announcement

Usually, the oral board has one or both of these to guide them. The qualities, characteristics or knowledges required by the position sought are stated in these documents. They offer valuable clues as to the nature of the oral interview. For example, if the job involves supervisory responsibilities, the announcement will usually indicate that knowledge of modern supervisory methods and the qualifications of the candidate as a supervisor will be tested. If so, you can expect such questions, frequently in the form of a hypothetical situation which you are expected to solve. NEVER go into an oral without knowledge of the duties and responsibilities of the job you seek.

### 3) Think through each qualification required

Try to visualize the kind of questions you would ask if you were a board member. How well could you answer them? Try especially to appraise your own knowledge and background in each area, *measured against the job sought*, and identify any areas in which you are weak. Be critical and realistic – do not flatter yourself.

### 4) Do some general reading in areas in which you feel you may be weak

For example, if the job involves supervision and your past experience has NOT, some general reading in supervisory methods and practices, particularly in the field of human relations, might be useful. Do NOT study agency procedures or detailed manuals. The oral board will be testing your understanding and capacity, not your memory.

### 5) Get a good night's sleep and watch your general health and mental attitude

You will want a clear head at the interview. Take care of a cold or any other minor ailment, and of course, no hangovers.

*What should be done on the day of the interview?*

Now comes the day of the interview itself. Give yourself plenty of time to get there. Plan to arrive somewhat ahead of the scheduled time, particularly if your appointment is in the fore part of the day. If a previous candidate fails to appear, the board might be ready for you a bit early. By early afternoon an oral board is almost invariably behind schedule if there are many candidates, and you may have to wait. Take along a book or magazine to read, or your application to review, but leave any extraneous material in the waiting room when you go in for your interview. In any event, relax and compose yourself.

The matter of dress is important. The board is forming impressions about you – from your experience, your manners, your attitude, and your appearance. Give your personal appearance careful attention. Dress your best, but not your flashiest. Choose conservative, appropriate clothing, and be sure it is immaculate. This is a business interview, and your appearance should indicate that you regard it as such. Besides, being well groomed and properly dressed will help boost your confidence.

Sooner or later, someone will call your name and escort you into the interview room. *This is it.* From here on you are on your own. It is too late for any more preparation. But remember, you asked for this opportunity to prove your fitness, and you are here because your request was granted.

*What happens when you go in?*

The usual sequence of events will be as follows: The clerk (who is often the board stenographer) will introduce you to the chairman of the oral board, who will introduce you to the other members of the board. Acknowledge the introductions before you sit down. Do not be surprised if you find a microphone facing you or a stenotypist sitting by. Oral interviews are usually recorded in the event of an appeal or other review.

Usually the chairman of the board will open the interview by reviewing the highlights of your education and work experience from your application – primarily for the benefit of the other members of the board, as well as to get the material into the record. Do not interrupt or comment unless there is an error or significant misinterpretation; if that is the case, do not hesitate. But do not quibble about insignificant matters. Also, he will usually ask you some question about your education, experience or your present job – partly to get you to start talking and to establish the interviewing "rapport." He may start the actual questioning, or turn it over to one of the other members. Frequently, each member undertakes the questioning on a particular area, one in which he is perhaps most competent, so you can expect each member to participate in the examination. Because time is limited, you may also expect some rather abrupt switches in the direction the questioning takes, so do not be upset by it. Normally, a board member will not pursue a single line of questioning unless he discovers a particular strength or weakness.

After each member has participated, the chairman will usually ask whether any member has any further questions, then will ask you if you have anything you wish to add. Unless you are expecting this question, it may floor you. Worse, it may start you off on an extended, extemporaneous speech. The board is not usually seeking more information. The question is principally to offer you a last opportunity to present further qualifications or to indicate that you have nothing to add. So, if you feel that a significant qualification or characteristic has been overlooked, it is proper to point it out in a sentence or so. Do not compliment the board on the thoroughness of their examination – they have been sketchy, and you know it. If you wish, merely say, "No thank you, I have nothing further to add." This is a point where you can "talk yourself out" of a good impression or fail to present an important bit of information. Remember, *you close the interview yourself*.

The chairman will then say, "That is all, Mr. _____, thank you." Do not be startled; the interview is over, and quicker than you think. Thank him, gather your belongings and take your leave. Save your sigh of relief for the other side of the door.

*How to put your best foot forward*

Throughout this entire process, you may feel that the board individually and collectively is trying to pierce your defenses, seek out your hidden weaknesses and embarrass and confuse you. Actually, this is not true. They are obliged to make an appraisal of your qualifications for the job you are seeking, and they want to see you in your best light. Remember, they must interview all candidates and a non-cooperative candidate may become a failure in spite of their best efforts to bring out his qualifications. Here are 15 suggestions that will help you:

**1) Be natural – Keep your attitude confident, not cocky**

If you are not confident that you can do the job, do not expect the board to be. Do not apologize for your weaknesses, try to bring out your strong points. The board is interested in a positive, not negative, presentation. Cockiness will antagonize any board member and make him wonder if you are covering up a weakness by a false show of strength.

**2) Get comfortable, but don't lounge or sprawl**

Sit erectly but not stiffly. A careless posture may lead the board to conclude that you are careless in other things, or at least that you are not impressed by the importance of the occasion. Either conclusion is natural, even if incorrect. Do not fuss with your clothing, a pencil or an ashtray. Your hands may occasionally be useful to emphasize a point; do not let them become a point of distraction.

**3) Do not wisecrack or make small talk**

This is a serious situation, and your attitude should show that you consider it as such. Further, the time of the board is limited – they do not want to waste it, and neither should you.

**4) Do not exaggerate your experience or abilities**

In the first place, from information in the application or other interviews and sources, the board may know more about you than you think. Secondly, you probably will not get away with it. An experienced board is rather adept at spotting such a situation, so do not take the chance.

**5) If you know a board member, do not make a point of it, yet do not hide it**

Certainly you are not fooling him, and probably not the other members of the board. Do not try to take advantage of your acquaintanceship – it will probably do you little good.

**6) Do not dominate the interview**

Let the board do that. They will give you the clues – do not assume that you have to do all the talking. Realize that the board has a number of questions to ask you, and do not try to take up all the interview time by showing off your extensive knowledge of the answer to the first one.

**7) Be attentive**

You only have 20 minutes or so, and you should keep your attention at its sharpest throughout. When a member is addressing a problem or question to you, give him your undivided attention. Address your reply principally to him, but do not exclude the other board members.

**8) Do not interrupt**

A board member may be stating a problem for you to analyze. He will ask you a question when the time comes. Let him state the problem, and wait for the question.

**9) Make sure you understand the question**

Do not try to answer until you are sure what the question is. If it is not clear, restate it in your own words or ask the board member to clarify it for you. However, do not haggle about minor elements.

**10) Reply promptly but not hastily**

A common entry on oral board rating sheets is "candidate responded readily," or "candidate hesitated in replies." Respond as promptly and quickly as you can, but do not jump to a hasty, ill-considered answer.

**11) Do not be peremptory in your answers**

A brief answer is proper – but do not fire your answer back. That is a losing game from your point of view. The board member can probably ask questions much faster than you can answer them.

**12) Do not try to create the answer you think the board member wants**

He is interested in what kind of mind you have and how it works – not in playing games. Furthermore, he can usually spot this practice and will actually grade you down on it.

**13) Do not switch sides in your reply merely to agree with a board member**

Frequently, a member will take a contrary position merely to draw you out and to see if you are willing and able to defend your point of view. Do not start a debate, yet do not surrender a good position. If a position is worth taking, it is worth defending.

### 14) Do not be afraid to admit an error in judgment if you are shown to be wrong

The board knows that you are forced to reply without any opportunity for careful consideration. Your answer may be demonstrably wrong. If so, admit it and get on with the interview.

### 15) Do not dwell at length on your present job

The opening question may relate to your present assignment. Answer the question but do not go into an extended discussion. You are being examined for a *new* job, not your present one. As a matter of fact, try to phrase ALL your answers in terms of the job for which you are being examined.

*Basis of Rating*

Probably you will forget most of these "do's" and "don'ts" when you walk into the oral interview room. Even remembering them all will not ensure you a passing grade. Perhaps you did not have the qualifications in the first place. But remembering them will help you to put your best foot forward, without treading on the toes of the board members.

Rumor and popular opinion to the contrary notwithstanding, an oral board wants you to make the best appearance possible. They know you are under pressure – but they also want to see how you respond to it as a guide to what your reaction would be under the pressures of the job you seek. They will be influenced by the degree of poise you display, the personal traits you show and the manner in which you respond.


## ABOUT THIS BOOK

This book contains tests divided into Examination Sections. Go through each test, answering every question in the margin. We have also attached a sample answer sheet at the back of the book that can be removed and used. At the end of each test look at the answer key and check your answers. On the ones you got wrong, look at the right answer choice and learn. Do not fill in the answers first. Do not memorize the questions and answers, but understand the answer and principles involved. On your test, the questions will likely be different from the samples. Questions are changed and new ones added. If you understand these past questions you should have success with any changes that arise. Tests may consist of several types of questions. We have additional books on each subject should more study be advisable or necessary for you. Finally, the more you study, the better prepared you will be. This book is intended to be the last thing you study before you walk into the examination room. Prior study of relevant texts is also recommended. NLC publishes some of these in our Fundamental Series. Knowledge and good sense are important factors in passing your exam. Good luck also helps. So now study this Passbook, absorb the material contained within and take that knowledge into the examination. Then do your best to pass that exam.

# EXAMINATION SECTION

# EXAMINATION SECTION
## TEST 1

DIRECTIONS: Each question or incomplete statement is followed by several suggested answers or completions. Select the one that BEST answers the question or completes the statement. *PRINT THE LETTER OF THE CORRECT ANSWER IN THE SPACE AT THE RIGHT.*

1. You are preparing a press release announcing a cornerstone laying ceremony for a housing project named after a prominent New Yorker. You desire to include in this press release some information about this person's contributions to public housing.
   Of the following sources which are available to you, the BEST one to go to in order to obtain verified information is
   A. the index and issues of a local newspaper obtainable in the public library
   B. Wikipedia
   C. a book on the history of public housing
   D. a biography of the individual

   1.____

2. You have been assigned to prepare a press release announcing the issuance of applications for apartments at a new city housing project.
   Of the following items of information, the one which is LEAST important to include in such a press release is the
   A. average building cost per apartment
   B. rental charges per room
   C. number of apartments in the project
   D. special facilities available at the project

   2.____

3. A company executive has asked you to assist him in preparing a presentation he is to deliver at a city board meeting concerning the potential benefits of a new government computer system. Members of the city administration will be present, as well as the press and the general public.
   Of the following, the theme you should emphasize MOST in this presentation is
   A. faster load times and stronger WiFi in all government buildings
   B. the inadequacies of the current computer system
   C. more efficient processing of city permits, payments and other transactions between the city and residents
   D. benefits of a digitally connected community

   3.____

4. You have been assigned to prepare a nightlife brochure that is to include photos of people dining at area restaurants. However, the photos you have are not adequate, so you run an image search on Google and find more suitable photos to use in the brochure.
   This practice is generally unacceptable because

   4.____

A. readers might notice that the people in the images are not actually dining at area restaurants
B. information on Google is not properly fact-checked
C. photos published on the internet cannot be used in print publications
D. use of the images might violate copyright law

5. It is your job to promote the fact that all pumpkins to be sold at an upcoming Fall Festival are harvested from local farms. Which of the following is the most effective way to ensure residents of the community are aware of this?
   A. Post notes on Twitter and Instagram, and tag the associated farms
   B. Run a print and online "Buy Local" campaign in the weeks leading up to the festival
   C. Publish a series of farmer profiles in the community newspaper
   D. Hang banners over local roads highlighting the festival and its amenities

5.____

6. Which of the following, about the opening of a new village dog park, is MOST appropriate according to standard rules of headline writing?
   A. YELPS OF DELIGHT YESTERDAY AS NEW DOG PARK OPENS TO CROWD OF 30 PUPS
   B. NEW FAIRMOUNT DOG PARK OFF TO "RUFF" START
   C. DOGGIE DESTINATION OPENED YESTERDAY IN FAIRMOUNT
   D. MORE BARK THAN BITE: DOG PARK OPENS IN FAIRMOUNT TO HOWLS OF GLORY FROM PUPS AND THEIR OWNERS

6.____

7. Suppose that you are assigned to release department information to reporters for the metropolitan press.
   Of the following, the LEAST desirable practice for you to adopt in this assignment is
   A. as a general rule, release information in written form only
   B. set regular dates for the release of department news insofar as possible
   C. secure clearance for the issuance of all written releases
   D. release information first to reporters for newspapers which give the best coverage to department news

7.____

8. A letter from a private citizen, complaining about a department policy which has worked a hardship on him, has been referred to you for reply. The citizen asks that this policy be changed.
   In answering this letter, it would be BEST to give major emphasis to
   A. an explanation of the reasons which make such a policy necessary
   B. pointing out that the department regulations cannot be revised to suit each individual case
   C. stating that the operations of any large organization must result in some hardships
   D. inducing the individual to come into the office where the matter can better be dealt with in a face-to-face interview

8.____

9. Suppose you are assigned to prepare the annual report for your department. Each bureau has been asked to submit a written report on its activities for the preceding year.
   Of the following, the MOST desirable action for you to take in carrying out this assignment is to
   A. return to the bureau heads for revision those reports which, in your opinion, contain unimportant material
   B. rewrite the material submitted by the bureaus to secure improved style without changing content
   C. arrange a conference with the bureau heads to discuss the reports they are to submit
   D. write an introduction and conclusion and let the reports of the bureaus constitute, unaltered, the body of the annual report

10. You have been assigned by your supervisor to do the preliminary editing of material written by other information assistants. After a week in this assignment, you evaluate the material submitted by one information assistant as of lower quality than that of the others.
    Of the following, the BEST action for you to take is to
    A. analyze his work with the other information assistants
    B. continue to edit his work without comment at this time
    C. suggest to him that he take a refresher course in writing
    D. recommend his transfer to less original work

11. You have completed gathering the necessary data for a routine newspaper release you are to write.
    The MOST desirable step for you to take next is to
    A. write a first draft of the release
    B. work out a plan for the release, including the beginning, the main points, and the ending
    C. develop a suitable title and then begin to write
    D. have someone familiar with the field check the accuracy of the data which you have gathered

12. Of the following writing techniques, the one which is generally LEAST effective for making written material more forceful is the
    A. repetition of a key word or phrase
    B. liberal use of exclamation points, capitalization, underlining and other similar devices
    C. use of the verbs in the active voice, rather than the passive voice
    D. use of a brief sentence, rather than a longer one, to express the same idea

13. The use of anecdotes and other verbal illustrations in writing is desirable PRIMARILY because
    A. this is a good way of showing the author's interest in his subject
    B. the reader will remember the anecdotes
    C. the illustrations will help the reader to remember the author's main idea
    D. the illustrations will entertain the reader

14. You are sending an e-mail to local community groups alerting them to a new youth sports program in municipal parks. It is considered good practice to include links to the department's social media accounts because
    A. it is an opportunity to gain more followers
    B. people respond more favorably to social media links
    C. sports programs are a popular topic on social media
    D. it provides additional outlets for readers to find detailed program information

15. The one of the following which is considered LEAST important in good news-writing is
    A. complete accuracy of names and addresses
    B. full identification of sources of information
    C. strict chronological order of presentation
    D. avoiding the use of editorial statements

16. Of the following, the BEST procedure to follow when writing an article to be read by experts is to
    A. avoid the technical terms as far as possible
    B. explain the technical terms the first time they are used
    C. use the technical terms of the experts
    D. use your literary judgment as to whether to use the technical terms

17. Of the following, the purpose for which it is LEAST important for a writer to have a large vocabulary is to
    A. give him a wider choice of synonyms and antonyms
    B. enable him to express himself in a sophisticated language
    C. improve his reading comprehension
    D. make his writing more exact

18. "The family lived in a small edifice on Maple Street."
    The preceding sentence involves a
    A. good choice of words
    B. poor choice of words because an "edifice" is large rather than small
    C. poor choice of words because the word "edifice" is obsolete
    D. poor choice of words because the word "edifice" is unfamiliar to the average reader

19. In fiction, the BEST way of acquainting the reader with the traits of the characters is through
    A. action
    B. dialogue and description
    C. action and dialogue
    D. dialogue

20. Subheads in an informal pamphlet
    A. are a matter of individual preference
    B. are appropriate only if the subject readily breaks itself down into separate sections
    C. should be used because the pamphlet will be easier to read
    D. should NOT be used because they look "textbookish"

21. The length of an average paragraph should
    A. be about 300 words
    B. harmonize with other elements of a writer's style
    C. not fall below 60 words
    D. vary according to each writing assignment

    21.____

22. In writing an informational blog post for young readers, it is advisable to include which of the following in order to hold readers' attention?
    A. Bulleted lists
    B. Links to relevant Twitter posts
    C. YouTube and TikTok videos
    D. All of the above

    22.____

23. Fictitious characters in factual writing should
    A. be disguised to make them appear real
    B. be given names rather than symbols
    C. be given symbols, such as A, B, and C, rather than names
    D. not be used

    23.____

24. "Clichés should be avoided in writing."
    The one of the following which is NOT a cliché is
    A. "every Tom, Dick and Harry"
    B. "left no stone unturned"
    C. "outrageous possibilities"
    D. "strike while the iron is hot"

    24.____

25. Public polling indicates that the majority of the American people are unacquainted with such items of general and historical information as the United Nations, the Enron scandal and the Y2K scare.
    Of the following, the MOST probable cause for this lack of knowledge is that
    A. people generally don't read enough to grasp this information
    B. most people don't know anything about current events or international relations
    C. schools avoid the teaching of controversial subjects
    D. this news was not dealt with in the newspapers read by the people polled

    25.____

26. The *Readers' Guide to Periodical Literature* is
    A. a digit of magazine articles
    B. a literary magazine
    C. an index of magazine articles
    D. an annual guide to magazines

    26.____

27. To publicize a senior citizens' golf outing hosted by the village parks department, you would likely reach the highest volume of interested participants by running a
    A. Facebook post targeted to seniors living in the state
    B. potentially viral TikTok video
    C. full-page ad in the village newspaper
    D. newspaper profile of the local golf pro

    27.____

28. All of the following are terms associated with publishing software EXCEPT
    A. point size
    B. click-through rate
    C. stock templates
    D. ePub

    28.____

29. Your department budget allocated $25,000 this year to be used specifically for digital marketing and promotion. Your supervisor has instructed you to use the money to update and modernize the department's web presence and increase reach. Of the following, the best use of these funds would be to
    A. set up a weekly podcast that features members of the community and how their work relates to the department
    B. improve SEO so that information about the department is more visible when community residents search for it
    C. hire a web designer to lay out a new website
    D. create an ongoing social media campaign that focuses on photos and short videos related to department functions and events in the community

    29.____

30. The e-mail field used to send a press release to 50 local journalists is
    A. To    B. CC    C. Incognito    D. BCC

    30.____

31. Of the following sentences, the one which is poorly written because it contains a "dangling construction" is:
    A. After waiting half an hour for the bus, I remembered that I had no money for carfare.
    B. Having returned from our vacations, the supervisor made reassignments.
    C. Smiling pleasantly, she acknowledged the applause of the audience.
    D. Walking over to him, I introduced myself and offered to help him catch his assailant.

    31.____

Questions 32-36.

DIRECTIONS: Questions 32 through 36 consist of three sentences each. For each question, select the sentence which contains NO error in grammar or usage and write the capital letter preceding that sentence in the space at the right.

32. A. Be sure that everybody brings his notes to the conference.
    B. He looked like he meant to hit the boy.
    C. Mr. Jones is one of the clients who was chosen to represent the district.
    D. All are incorrect.

    32.____

33. A. He is taller than I.
    B. I'll have nothing to do with these kind of people.
    C. The reason why he will not buy the house is because it is too expensive.
    D. All are incorrect.

    33.____

34. A. Aren't I eligible for this apartment.
    B. Have you seen him anywheres?
    C. He should of come earlier.
    D. All are incorrect.

    34.____

35. A. He graduated college in 1982.
    B. He hadn't but one more line to write.
    C. Who do you think is the author of this report?
    D. All are incorrect.

    35.____

36. A. I talked to one official, whom I knew was fully impartial.
    B. Everyone signed the petition but him.
    C. He proved not only to be a good student but also a good athlete.
    D. All are incorrect.

36.____

Questions 37-40.

DIRECTIONS: Questions 37 through 40 consist of three sentences each. For each item, select the sentence which contains NO error in word usage and write the capital letter preceding that sentence in the space at the right.

37. A. Every year a large amount of tenants are admitted to housing projects.
    B. Henry Ford owned around a billion dollars in industrial equipment.
    C. He was aggravated by the child's bead behavior.
    D. All are incorrect.

37.____

38. A. Before he was committed to the asylum he suffered from the illusion that he was Napoleon.
    B. Besides stocks, there were also bonds in the safe.
    C. We bet the other team easily.
    D. All are incorrect.

38.____

39. A. Bring this report to your supervisor immediately.
    B. He set the chair down near the table.
    C. The capitol of New York is Albany.
    D. All are incorrect.

39.____

40. A. He was chosen to arbitrate the dispute because everyone knew he would be disinterested.
    B. It is advisable to obtain the best council before making an important decision,
    C. Less college students are interested in teaching than ever before.
    D. All are incorrect.

40.____

## KEY (CORRECT ANSWERS)

| | | | | | | | |
|---|---|---|---|---|---|---|---|
| 1. | D | 11. | B | 21. | D | 31. | B |
| 2. | A | 12. | B | 22. | D | 32. | A |
| 3. | C | 13. | C | 23. | B | 33. | A |
| 4. | D | 14. | D | 24. | C | 34. | D |
| 5. | B | 15. | C | 25. | A | 35. | C |
| 6. | B | 16. | C | 26. | C | 36. | B |
| 7. | D | 17. | B | 27. | C | 37. | D |
| 8. | A | 18. | B | 28. | B | 38. | B |
| 9. | C | 19. | C | 29. | D | 39. | B |
| 10. | B | 20. | C | 30. | D | 40. | A |

# TEST 2

DIRECTIONS: Each question or incomplete statement is followed by several suggested answers or completions. Select the one that BEST answers the question or completes the statement. *PRINT THE LETTER OF THE CORRECT ANSWER IN THE SPACE AT THE RIGHT.*

1. "Study your audience and slant your writing toward it." 1.____
 Of the following, the BEST procedure to adopt in applying this principle is to
 A. estimate the intelligence of your audience and write accordingly
 B. use the simplest possible prose style
 C. write about the things you believe your audience wants to read, rather than the things you would prefer to write about
 D. write about what you want to say in the form that is most likely to appeal to your audience

2. "The first rule for giving your writing 'punch' is to take the most important idea 2.____
 and save it until the end of the sentence."
 Of the following sentences, the one which BEST illustrates this principle is:
 A. After they had notified the police, and had searched the entire neighborhood for hours, they found the little girl in the attic, sleeping peacefully.
 B. The enemy has destroyed the lives of our people, plundered our seas, ravaged our coasts, and burnt our towns.
 C. The thief had stolen the top-secret report, broken open the safe, and rifled the desk.
 D. The tornado left ruin and death in its wake and tore down every building in the village.

3. "America has been built by the cooperative effort of many different kinds of 3.____
 people, working together."
 In the preceding sentence, a word or phrase which is NOT made superfluous by the use of another word or phrase of similar meaning is
 A. different B. kinds of
 C. many D. working together

4. "The company did so well this year that, at the end of the year, it gave each 4.____
 employee a carton of cigarettes, a bottle of wine, and – a $100 bond."
 In the preceding sentence, the dash
 A. adds more force to the words which follow
 B. detracts from the force of the words which follow
 C. is an illustration of the improper use of punctuation
 D. neither adds nor detracts from the force of the words which follow

5. An e-mail written by another information assistant begins with this sentence: 5.____
 "We beg to acknowledge your note sent to us on the 23rd." It then goes on to reply directly to the matters raised in the note of the 23rd.

If you are assigned to edit this e-mail for clarity, the MOST desirable action of the following for you to take is to
- A. change the first sentence to read: "We beg to acknowledge your note sent to us on the 23rd and in reply wish to state that...."
- B. leave the first sentence as it is
- C. leave the first sentence unchanged but add another immediately following summarizing what the note of the 23rd inquired about
- D. omit the first sentence in its entirety

6. "Write as you talk" is an axiom widely accepted by news writers. Newspaper readers have a better chance of grasping the news if it is told to them simply and clearly.
The MOST direct implication of the preceding statement is that
- A. an axiom is a statement whose truth is generally accepted by everyone
- B. flowery readers are no different from newspaper reporters
- C. newspaper readers are no different from newspaper reporters
- D. the use of ungrammatical constructions is sometimes justified in writing for the newspapers

6.\_\_\_\_

7. "Nowadays, lack of information usually goes hand in hand with little education; similarly, lack of information also usually goes hand in hand with low income. So, if you are writing for people in the lower income brackets or people who haven't gone to college, it's a good guess that they won't have much background knowledge."
The preceding statement implies MOST directly that
- A. little education has always been negatively correlated with little information
- B. poor people are usually not well-informed
- C. people who have not gone to college are in the lower income brackets
- D. writing for the poor and uneducated is more difficult than writing for the rich and well-educated

7.\_\_\_\_

8. "Prices of building materials are, in the aggregate, more rigid than those of other commodities. Concentration of control over the supply of goods is frequently advanced as the explanation for price rigidities in general and for building materials in particular."
According to the preceding statement,
- A. increased demand and concurrent fixed supply are frequently responsible for increased prices of building materials
- B. in the aggregate, the high cost of building materials contributes substantially to the high cost of new housing construction
- C. the cost of most articles is generally more flexible than the cost of articles required in the construction of new buildings
- D. the existence of faulty methods of distribution is often advanced as an argument to explain price inequities

8.\_\_\_\_

9. "In undertaking a new development, the builder first decides upon the price or rental range of the dwellings he proposes to construct. Then, after roughly estimating the cost of the selected structure, he tries to find land at suitable prices."
According to the preceding statement,
   A. after a new development is completed, the builder adds up his construction and land costs and fixes the price of the individual house accordingly
   B. it is difficult to predict the probable cost of a new dwelling unit because of constant fluctuation in the cost of building materials
   C. land costs influence the selling price of dwellings least
   D. the selling price of a house is usually determined before construction is begun

9.____

10. "A construction program initiated by public agencies better protects the home buyer and insures the greater soundness of the neighborhood."
According to the preceding statement,
   A. a home buyer is more confident of the safety of his investment if he is given to understand that the neighborhood will not change
   B. a public agency is more responsible in construction programs than a private builder could hope to be
   C. since a public agency can, if necessary, control the development of a neighborhood through zoning laws, public housing is more desirable
   D. to ensure the soundness of a neighborhood it is more effective to have the building of new homes planned by public agencies

10.____

11. "To achieve sound planning we cannot rely on educating the builder to the fact that what is good for the public will be ultimately good for him, for his interest is usually short term and the pattern in which he functions is not set up for voluntary reform."
According to the preceding statement,
   A. a builder is not interested in educating the public to its ultimate benefits
   B. builders whose interests are usually of short duration can be educated to set up voluntary reforms
   C. since a builder's interest in any property is usually of short duration, he will voluntarily function for public benefit
   D. we cannot rely on educating a builder to the fact that public benefit is to his advantage in the long run

11.____

12. "If cities had a long-range objective, if they had plans showing the expected line of growth, plans for their future schools and parks, their houses and their locations, their industries and their locations, their future transportation facilities and their utilities, then with the advent of an emergency requiring government spending they could channel the expenditures and step up the program along the lines of the larger long-term plans."

12.____

According to the preceding statement,
- A. a city wishing to eliminate slums can with proper planning take advantage of an emergency requiring the channeling of expenditures
- B. an emergency requires the channeling of expenditures so that greater efficiency can be shown in planning
- C. cities which have long-range plans can make better use of the funds spent by the government during a depression
- D. long-range objectives help a city to devise new plans for the development of parks, schools, and other public improvements at a considerable saving

13. "Increment or decrement in city income hangs largely upon the maintenance of the values and valuations of real property, upon the quantity of new improvements that go into the city, upon the profitableness of real estate, upon the advent of booms and depressions, and upon the flow of people into or out of the city."
    According to the preceding statement,
    - A. a boom or a depression has a marked effect on the flow of people into or out of a city
    - B. new improvements that go into a city enhance the profitableness of real estate
    - C. real estate values, which form the major basis of a city's taxation, are the sources of city salaries
    - D. the valuation of a city's income depends on the values of the real estate in the city

13.\_\_\_\_

14. "The institution of the family is a vitally important part of all human societies, but in modern society, particularly, various organized services have developed that enable some people to secure some of the most essential benefits of family life without belonging to a family group."
    Of the following, the LEAST valid inference on the basis of the preceding statement is that
    - A. people who are not part of a family unit can obtain most of the essential benefits of family life by contacting an appropriate social agency
    - B. present day society offers an opportunity to some who are not members of a family unit to share in some of the benefits of family living
    - C. the institution of the family is not native to modern society alone
    - D. to obtain the benefits of family life it is usually necessary to belong to a family group

14.\_\_\_\_

15. "Reform organizations seek, as a rule, to bring about a specific economic or political change; social work agencies are usually occupied with the task of meeting existing situations in the lives of particular individuals or groups."
    According to the preceding statement,
    - A. a reform organization is concerned with helping the individual by changing some factor in the environment which the individual feels is too arduous to accept
    - B. a reform organization is not concerned with the ability of the individual to meet his social responsibilities

15.\_\_\_\_

C. social work agencies are not concerned with any specific economic or political change because this does not involve the individual's personal adjustment
D. social workers are primarily concerned with helping their clients to meet current living conditions

16. "Adequate facilities for education, recreation and health must be provided for children, and social conditions created that promote the child's development into law-abiding citizens. It is not the task of social work to provide these facilities but to direct children to them and to help them to use these facilities."
Of the following, the MOST accurate statement on the basis of the preceding statement is that
    A. A child who does not have adequate educational, recreational and health facilities will develop into a poor citizen
    B. the education of the public to the importance of providing adequate facilities for children is primarily the social worker's responsibility
    C. the proper use of leisure time by children is an important aspect of the social worker's job
    D. the three most important needs of a child which must be satisfied first are those of education, recreation and health

16.____

17. "Social workers start from the assumption that preservation of the family as the basic unit of social living is their accepted objective. In view of the frequency of divorce and the breakdown of authority in the home, social work now makes articulate its concern for family integrity."
According to the preceding statement,
    A. failure to keep the family as a basic unit leads to a breakdown of authority in the home, upsetting family integrity
    B. in extreme cases where divorce is inevitable a social worker must accept the breakdown of the family unit
    C. social workers are primarily concerned with keeping a family together as a basis entity of social living
    D. the importance of the family to society has been demonstrated by experience with children who have been institutionalized

17.____

18. "The marked change in the spirit in which social work is carried on is evidenced in the adoption of business methods of organization, including centralized purchasing of supplies for social agencies, cost accounting, careful budgeting and auditing of accounts, evaluation of methods and publication of reports. Trained personnel for defined jobs is increasingly sought, and there is appreciation of the differentiated abilities required in the social agency."
According to the preceding statement,
    A. it is apparent that the adoption of business methods of organization has resulted in a change in the method of preparing case work reports
    B. social work agencies that train people for definite jobs achieve savings in social work that approximate those of business organization

18.____

C. social work now uses current business procedures in carrying forward the purposes of a social agency
D. trained personnel in social work are responsible for the adoption of business methods of procedure

19. "Basic to the functioning of the professional social worker is an understanding of human personality and of the world we live in."
The one of the following which is the MOST accurate statement on the basis of the preceding quotation is that
   A. a social worker must be familiar with human behavior in order to be able to perform his work properly
   B. a social worker who understands human personality is able to function better as a citizen of the world
   C. social work may be classified as a profession because, for its proper performance, a basic understanding of the social and biological sciences is required
   D. through his daily contact with his clients a social worker will obtain a better understanding of the world he lives in

19._____

Questions 20-24.

DIRECTIONS: Questions 20 through 24 each consist of three words. For each item, select the word which is INCORRECTLY spelled and write the capital letter preceding that word in the space at the right.

20. A. achievment         B. maintenance         20._____
    C. questionnaire      D. all are correct

21. A. prevelant          B. pronunciation       21._____
    C. separate           D. all are correct

22. A. permissible        B. relevant            22._____
    C. seize              D. all are correct

23. A. corroborate        B. desparate           23._____
    C. eighth             D. all are correct

24. A. exceed             B. feasibility         24._____
    C. psycological       D. all are correct

Questions 25-29.

DIRECTIONS: Questions 25 through 29 are to be answered on the basis of the following information.

Copy I is an accurate copy of material which is to be prepared for the printer. Copy II of this material contains a number of typographical errors. Compare Copy II with Copy I and find the typographical errors. Every group of four lines in Copy II is numbered. Indicate the number of typographical errors in each group of lines of Copy II by writing in the correspondingly numbered space at the right the capital letter preceding the best of the following alternatives.

- A. No errors
- B. 1-2 errors
- C. 3-4 errors
- D. 5 or more errors

COPY I

Parcel 1. Beginning at a point formed by the intersection of the northerly side of 73$^{rd}$ avenue with the westerly side of Francis Lewis boulevard as said streets are indicated upon the final map of the borough of Queens known as Alteration Map No. 2831 adopted by the board of estimate on May 15, 1941; running thence northerly along the westerly side of Francis Lewis boulevard following a curve having a radius of 8,053 feet for a distance of 585.15 feet; thence northerly along the westerly side of Francis Lewis boulevard in a straight line for a distance of 687.43 feet; thence northerly along the westerly side of Francis Lewis boulevard and its prolongation following a curve having a radius of 5.667 feet for a distance of 509.79 feet to the old southerly side of North Hempstead turnpike as formerly laid out and as shown discontinued upon the aforementioned final city map; thence easterly along said southerly side of North Hempstead turnpike for 110.12 feet to the easterly side of Francis Lewis boulevard; thence southerly along the easterly side of Francis Lewis boulevard following a curve having a radius of 5.783 feet for a distance of 489.20 feet; thence southerly along the easterly side of Francis Lewis boulevard in a straight line for a distance of 687.43 feet; thence southerly along the easterly side of Francis Lewis boulevard following a curve having a radius of 7,947 feet for a distance of 572.90 feet to the northerly side of 73$^{rd}$ avenue.

COPY II

25. Parcel 1. Beginning at point formed by the intersection of the northerly side of 73$^{rd}$ Avenue with the westerly side of Francis Lewis boulevard as said streets are indicated upon the final map of the borough of Queens known as Alteration Map No. 2831 adapted by the board of estimate on May15, 1941;

25.____

26. running thence northerly along the westerly side of Francis Lewis boulevard following a curve having a radius of 8,053 feet for a distance of 585.15 feet; thence northerly along the westerly side of Francis Lewis boulevard in a straight line for a distance of 687.43 feet; thence northerly along

26.____

27. the westerly side of Francis Lewis boulevard and its prolongation following a curve having a radius of 5.677 feet for a distance of 509.79 feet to the old southerly side of North Hempstead Turnpike as formerly laid out and is shown discontinued upon the aforementioned final city map; thence easterly

27.____

28. along said southerly side of North Hempstead turnpike for 1101.2 feet to the easterly side of Francis Lewis boulevard; thence southerly along the easterly side of Francis Lewis boulevard following a curve having a radius of 5.783 feet for a distance of 489.20 feet; thence southerly along the easterly

28.____

29. side of Francis Lewis boulevard in a straight line for a distance of 687.43 feet; thence southerly along the easterly side of Francis Lewis boulevard following a curve having a radius of 7,947 feet for a distance of 572.09 feet to the northerly side of 73rd avenue.

29.____

30. "He described a hypothetical situation to illustrate his point."
In the preceding sentence, the word "hypothetical" means MOST NEARLY
   A. actual    B. theoretical    C. typical    D. unusual

30.____

31. "I gave tacit approval to my partner's proposed business changes."
In the preceding sentence, the word "tacit" means MOST NEARLY
   A. enthusiastic    B. partial    C. silent    D. written

31.____

32. "Jones was considered an astute lawyer by the members of his profession."
In the preceding sentence, the word "astute" means MOST NEARLY
   A. clever    B. persevering
   C. poorly trained    D. unethical

32.____

33. "There were intimations even in early days of the way in which he would go."
In the preceding sentence, the word "intimations" means MOST NEARLY
   A. hints    B. patterns    C. plans    D. purposes

33.____

34. "His last book was published posthumously."
In the preceding sentence, the word "posthumously" means MOST NEARLY
   A. after the death of the author    B. printed free by the publisher
   C. without a dedication    D. without royalties

34.____

35. "When he was challenged, he used every known subterfuge."
In the preceding sentence, the word "subterfuge" means MOST NEARLY
   A. evasion to justify one's conduct
   B. means of attack to defend one's self
   C. medical device
   D. unconscious thought

35.____

36. "His partner suggested a course of action that would alleviate the difficulties which confronted him."
In the preceding sentence, the word "alleviate" means MOST NEARLY
   A. correct    B. lessen    C. remove    D. solve

36.____

37. "Among the applicants for the new apartment white-collar workers were preponderant."
In the preceding sentence, the word "preponderant" means MOST NEARLY
   A. considered not eligible    B. in evidence
   C. superior in number    D. the first to apply

37.____

38. "The captain gave a lucid explanation of his plans for the coming campaign."  38.____
    In the preceding sentence, the word "lucid" means MOST NEARLY
    A. clear    B. graphic    C. interesting    D. thorough

39. "He led a sedentary life."  39.____
    In the preceding sentence, the word "sedentary" means MOST NEARLY
    A. aimless    B. exciting    C. full    D. inactive

40. "His plan for the next campaign was very plausible."  40.____
    In the preceding sentence, the word "plausible" means MOST NEARLY
    A. appropriate    B. believable    C. usable    D. valuable

---

# KEY (CORRECT ANSWERS)

| | | | | | | | |
|---|---|---|---|---|---|---|---|
| 1. | D | 11. | D | 21. | A | 31. | C |
| 2. | A | 12. | C | 22. | D | 32. | A |
| 3. | C | 13. | D | 23. | B | 33. | A |
| 4. | A | 14. | A | 24. | C | 34. | A |
| 5. | D | 15. | D | 25. | C | 35. | A |
| 6. | B | 16. | C | 26. | A | 36. | B |
| 7. | B | 17. | C | 27. | C | 37. | C |
| 8. | C | 18. | C | 28. | B | 38. | A |
| 9. | D | 19. | A | 29. | B | 39. | D |
| 10. | D | 20. | A | 30. | B | 40. | B |

# EXAMINATION SECTION
## TEST 1

DIRECTIONS: Each question or incomplete statement is followed by several suggested answers or completions. Select the one that BEST answers the question or completes the statement. *PRINT THE LETTER OF THE CORRECT ANSWER IN THE SPACE AT THE RIGHT.*

1. When conducting a needs assessment for the purpose of education planning, an agency's FIRST step is to identify or provide
    A. a profile of population characteristics
    B. barriers to participation
    C. existing resources
    D. profiles of competing resources

    1._____

2. Research has demonstrated that of the following, the MOST effective medium for communicating with external publics is(are)
    A. video news releases   B. television
    C. radio                 D. newspapers

    2._____

3. Basic ideas behind the effort to influence the attitudes and behaviors of a constituency include each of the following EXCEPT the idea that
    A. words, rather than actions or events, are most likely to motivate
    B. demands for action are a usual response
    C. self-interest usually figures heavily into public involvement
    D. the reliability of change programs is difficult to assess

    3._____

4. An agency representative is trying to craft a pithy message to constituents in order to encourage the use of agency program resources.
   Choosing an audience for such messages is easiest when the message
    A. is project- or behavior-based   B. is combined with other messages
    C. is abstract                     D. has a broad appeal

    4._____

5. Of the following factors, the MOST important to the success of an agency's external education or communication programs is the
    A. amount of resources used to implement them
    B. public's prior experiences with the agency
    C. real value of the program to the public
    D. commitment of the internal audience

    5._____

6. A representative for a state agency is being interviewed by a reporter from a local news network. The representative is being asked to defend a program that is extremely unpopular in certain parts of the municipality.
   When a constituency is known to be opposed to a position, the MOST useful communication strategy is to present

    6._____

A. only the arguments that are consistent with constituents' views
B. only the agency's side of the issue
C. both sides of the argument as clearly as possible
D. both sides of the argument, omitting key information about the opposing position

7. The MOST significant barriers to effective agency community relations include
   I. widespread distrust of communication strategies
   II. the media's "watchdog" stance
   III. public apathy
   IV. statutory opposition

   The CORRECT answer is:
   A. I only      B. I and II      C. II and III      D. III and IV

8. In conducting an education program, many agencies use workshops and seminars in a classroom setting.
   Advantages of classroom-style teaching over other means of educating the public include each of the following, EXCEPT
   A. enabling an instructor to verify learning through testing and interaction with the target audience
   B. enabling hands-on practice and other participatory learning techniques
   C. ability to reach an unlimited number of participants in a given length of time
   D. ability to convey the latest, most up-to-date information

9. The _____ model of community relations is characterized by an attempt to persuade the public to adopt the agency's point of view.
   A. two-way symmetric         B. two-way asymmetric
   C. public information        D. press agency/publicity

10. Important elements of an internal situation analysis include the
    I. list of agency opponents        II. communication audit
    III. updated organizational almanac   IV. stakeholder analysis

    The CORRECT answer is:
    A. I and II      B. I, II, and III      C. II and III      D. I, II, III and IV

11. Government agency information efforts typically involve each of the following objectives, EXCEPT to
    A. implement changes in the policies of government agencies to align with public opinion
    B. communicate the work of agencies
    C. explain agency techniques in a way that invites input from citizens
    D. provide citizen feedback to government administrators

12. Factors that are likely to influence the effectiveness of an educational campaign include the
    I. level of homogeneity among intended participants
    II. number and types of media used
    III. receptivity of the intended participants
    IV. level of specificity in the message or behavior to be taught

    The CORRECT answer is:
    A. I and II    B. I, II, and III    C. II and III    D. I, II, III, and IV

13. An agency representative is writing instructional objectives that will later help to measure the effectiveness of an educational program.
    Which of the following verbs, included in an objective, would be MOST helpful for the purpose of measuring effectiveness?
    A. Know    B. Identify    C. Learn    D. Comprehend

14. A state education agency wants to encourage participation in a program that has just received a boost through new federal legislation. The program is intended to include participants from a wide variety of socioeconomic and other demographic characteristics. The agency wants to launch a broad-based program that will inform virtually every interested party in the state about the program's new circumstances.
    In attempting to deliver this message to such a wide-ranging constituency, the agency's BEST practice would be to
    A. broadcast the same message through as many different media channels as possible
    B. focus on one discrete segment of the public at a time
    C. craft a message whose appeal is as broad as the public itself
    D. let the program's achievements speak for themselves and rely on word-of-mouth

15. Advantages associated with using the World Wide Web as an educational tool include
    I. an appeal to younger generations of the public
    II. visually-oriented, interactive learning
    III. learning that is not confined by space, time, or institutional association
    IV. a variety of methods for verifying use and learning

    The CORRECT answer is:
    A. I only    B. I and II    C. I, II, and III    D. I, II, II, and IV

16. In agencies involved in health care, community relations is a critical function because it
    A. serves as an intermediary between the agency and consumers
    B. generates a clear mission statement for agency goals and priorities
    C. ensures patient privacy while satisfying the media's right to information
    D. helps marketing professionals determine the wants and needs of agency constituents

17. After an extensive campaign to promote its newest program to constituents, an agency learns that most of the audience did not understand the intended message.
MOST likely, the agency has
   A. chosen words that were intended to inform, rather than persuade
   B. not accurately interpreted what the audience really needed to know
   C. overestimated the ability of the audience to receive and process the message
   D. compensated for noise that may have interrupted the message

18. The necessary elements that lead to conviction and motivation in the minds of participants in an educational or information program include each of the following, EXCEPT the _____ of the message.
   A. acceptability            B. intensity
   C. single-channel appeal    D. pervasiveness

19. Printed materials are often at the core of educational programs provided by public agencies.
The PRIMARY disadvantage associated with print is that it
   A. does not enable comprehensive treatment of a topic
   B. is generally unreliable in term of assessing results
   C. is often the most expensive medium available
   D. is constrained by time

20. Traditional thinking on public opinion holds that there is about _____ percent of the public who are pivotal to shifting the balance and momentum of opinion—they are concerned about an issue, but not fanatical, and interested enough to pay attention to a reasoned discussion.
   A. 2        B. 10        C. 33        D. 51

21. One of the most useful guidelines for influencing attitude change among people is to
   A. invite the target audience to come to you, rather than approaching them
   B. use moral appeals as the primary approach
   C. use concrete images to enable people to see the results of behaviors or indifference
   D. offer tangible rewards to people for changes in behavior

22. An agency is attempting to evaluate the effectiveness of its educational program. For this purpose, it wants to observe several focus groups discussing the same program.
Which of the following would NOT be a guideline for the use of focus groups?
   A. Focus groups should only include those who have participated in the program.
   B. Be sure to accurately record the discussion.
   C. The same questions should be asked at each focus group meeting.
   D. It is often helpful to have a neutral, non-agency employee facilitate discussions.

23. Research consistently shows that _____ is the determinant most likely to make a newspaper editor run a news release.
    A. novelty   B. prominence   C. proximity   D. conflict

24. Which of the following is NOT one of the major variables to take into account when considering a population-needs assessment?
    A. State of program development   B. Resources available
    C. Demographics                   D. Community attitudes

25. The FIRST step in any communications audit is to
    A. develop a research instrument
    B. determine how the organization currently communicates
    C. hire a contractor
    D. determine which audience to assess

## KEY (CORRECT ANSWERS)

| | | | | |
|---|---|---|---|---|
| 1. | A | | 11. | A |
| 2. | D | | 12. | D |
| 3. | A | | 13. | B |
| 4. | A | | 14. | B |
| 5. | D | | 15. | C |
| | | | | |
| 6. | C | | 16. | A |
| 7. | D | | 17. | B |
| 8. | C | | 18. | C |
| 9. | B | | 19. | B |
| 10. | C | | 20. | B |

21. C
22. A
23. C
24. C
25. D

# TEST 2

DIRECTIONS: Each question or incomplete statement is followed by several suggested answers or completions. Select the one that BEST answers the question or completes the statement. *PRINT THE LETTER OF THE CORRECT ANSWER IN THE SPACE AT THE RIGHT.*

1. A public relations practitioner at an agency has just composed a press release highlighting a program's recent accomplishments and success stories.
   In pitching such releases to print outlets, the practitioner should
   I. e-mail, mail, or send them by messenger
   II. address them to "editor" or "news director"
   III. have an assistant call all media contacts by telephone
   IV. ask reporters or editors how they prefer to receive them

   The CORRECT answer is:
   A. I and II  B. I and IV  C. II, III, and IV  D. III only

2. The "output goals" of an educational program are MOST likely to include
   A. specified ratings of services by participants on a standardized scale
   B. observable effects on a given community or clientele
   C. the number of instructional hours provided
   D. the number of participants served

3. An agency wants to evaluate satisfaction levels among program participants, and mails out questionnaires to everyone who has been enrolled in the last year.
   The PRIMARY problem associated with this method of evaluative research is that it
   A. poses a significant inconvenience for respondents
   B. is inordinately expensive
   C. does not allow for follow-up or clarification questions
   D. usually involves a low response rate

4. A communications audit is an important tool for measuring
   A. the depth of penetration of a particular message or program
   B. the cost of the organization's information campaigns
   C. how key audiences perceive an organization
   D. the commitment of internal stakeholders

5. The "ABCs" of written learning objectives include each of the following, EXCEPT
   A. Audience  B. Behavior  C. Conditions  D. Delineation

6. When attempting to change the behaviors of constituents, it is important to keep in mind that
   I. most people are skeptical of communications that try to get them to change their behaviors
   II. in most cases, a person selects the media to which he exposes himself
   III. people tend to react defensively to messages or programs that rely on fear as a motivating factor
   IV. programs should aim for the broadest appeal possible in order to include as many participants as possible

   The CORRECT answer is:
   A. I and II   B. I, II and III   C. II and III   D. I, II, III, and IV

7. The "laws" of public opinion include the idea that it is
   A. useful for anticipating emergencies
   B. not sensitive to important events
   C. basically determined by self-interest
   D. sustainable through persistent appeals

8. Which of the following types of evaluations is used to measure public attitudes before and after an information/educational program?
   A. Retrieval study         B. Copy test
   C. Quota sampling          D. Benchmark study

9. The PRIMARY source for internal communications is(are) usually
   A. flow charts             B. meetings
   C. voice mail              D. printed publications

10. An agency representative is putting together informational materials—brochures and a newsletter—outlining changes in one of the state's biggest benefits programs.
    In assembling print materials as a medium for delivering information to the public, the representative should keep in mind each of the following trends:
    I. For various reasons, the reading capabilities of the public are in general decline
    II. Without tables and graphs to help illustrate the changes, it is unlikely that the message will be delivered effectively
    III. Professionals and career-oriented people are highly receptive to information written in the form of a journal article or empirical study
    IV. People tend to be put off by print materials that use itemized and bulleted (●) lists

    The CORRECT answer is:
    A. I and II   B. I, II and III   C. II and III   D. I, II, III, and IV

11. Which of the following steps in a problem-oriented information campaign would typically be implemented FIRST?
    A. Deciding on tactics
    B. Determining a communications strategy
    C. Evaluating the problem's impact
    D. Developing an organizational strategy

11._____

12. A common pitfall in conducting an educational program is to
    A. aim it at the wrong target audience
    B. overfund it
    C. leave it in the hands of people who are in the business of education, rather than those with expertise in the business of the organization
    D. ignore the possibility that some other organization is meeting the same educational need for the target audience

12._____

13. The key factors that affect the credibility of an agency's educational program include
    A. organization            B. scope
    C. sophistication          D. penetration

13._____

14. Research on public opinion consistently demonstrates that it is
    A. easy to move people toward a strong opinion on anything, as long as they are approached directly through their emotions
    B. easier to move people away from an opinion they currently hold than to have them form an opinion about something they have not previously cared about
    C. easy to move people toward a strong opinion on anything, as long as the message appeals to their reason and intellect
    D. difficult to move people toward a strong opinion on anything, no matter what the approach

14._____

15. In conducting an education program, many agencies use meetings and conferences to educate an audience about the organization and its programs. Advantages associated with this approach include
    I. a captive audience that is known to be interested in the topic
    II. ample opportunities for verifying learning
    III. cost-efficient meeting space
    IV. the ability to provide information on a wider variety of subjects

    The CORRECT answer is:
    A. I and II     B. I, III and IV     C. II and III     D. I, II, III and IV

15._____

16. An agency is attempting to evaluate the effectiveness of its educational programs. For this purpose, it wants to observe several focus groups discussing particular programs.
    For this purpose, a focus group should never number more than _____ participants.
    A. 5           B. 10          C. 15          D. 20

16._____

17. A _____ speech is written so that several agency members can deliver it to different audiences with only minor variations.
    A. basic   B. printed   C. quota   D. pattern

18. Which of the following statements about public opinion is generally considered to be FALSE?
    A. Opinion is primarily reactive rather than proactive.
    B. People have more opinions about goals than about the means by which to achieve them.
    C. Facts tend to shift opinion in the accepted direction when opinion is not solidly structured.
    D. Public opinion is based more on information than desire.

19. An agency is trying to promote its educational program.
    As a general rule, the agency should NOT assume that
    A. people will only participate if they perceive an individual benefit
    B. promotions need to be aimed at small, discrete groups
    C. if the program is good, the audience will find out about it
    D. a variety of methods, including advertising, special events, and direct mail, should be considered

20. In planning a successful educational program, probably the first and most important question for an agency to ask is:
    A. What will be the content of the program?
    B. Who will be served by the program?
    C. When is the best time to schedule the program?
    D. Why is the program necessary?

21. Media kits are LEAST likely to contain
    A. fact sheets            B. memoranda
    C. photographs with captions   D. news releases

22. The use of pamphlets and booklets as media for communication with the public often involves the disadvantage that
    A. the messages contained within them are frequently nonspecific
    B. it is difficult to measure their effectiveness in delivering the message
    C. there are few opportunities for people to refer to them
    D. color reproduction is poor

23. The MOST important prerequisite of a good educational program is an
    A. abundance of resources to implement it
    B. individual staff unit formed for the purpose of program delivery
    C. accurate needs assessment
    D. uneducated constituency

24. After an education program has been delivered, an agency conducts a program evaluation to determine whether its objectives have been met.
General rules about how to conduct such an education program valuation include each of the following, EXCEPT that it
   A. must be done immediately after the program has been implemented
   B. should be simple and easy to use
   C. should be designed so that tabulation of responses can take place quickly and inexpensively
   D. should solicit mostly subjective, open-ended responses if the audience was large

25. Using electronic media such as television as means of educating the public is typically recommended ONLY for agencies that
   I. have a fairly simple message to begin with
   II. want to reach the masses, rather than a targeted audience
   III. have substantial financial resources
   IV. accept that they will not be able to measure the results of the campaign with much precision

   The CORRECT answer is:
   A. I and II      B. I, II and III     C. II and IV     D. I, II, III and IV

## KEY (CORRECT ANSWERS)

| | | | | |
|---|---|---|---|---|
| 1. | B | | 11. | C |
| 2. | C | | 12. | D |
| 3. | D | | 13. | A |
| 4. | C | | 14. | D |
| 5. | D | | 15. | B |
| 6. | B | | 16. | B |
| 7. | C | | 17. | D |
| 8. | D | | 18. | D |
| 9. | D | | 19. | C |
| 10. | A | | 20. | D |

| | |
|---|---|
| 21. | B |
| 22. | B |
| 23. | C |
| 24. | D |
| 25. | D |

# EXAMINATION SECTION
# TEST 1

DIRECTIONS: Each question or incomplete statement is followed by several suggested answers or completions. Select the one that BEST answers the question or completes the statement. *PRINT THE LETTER OF THE CORRECT ANSWER IN THE SPACE AT THE RIGHT.*

1. A group member who starts out at the same level as other group members and is able to move into a leadership position within that group would be described as what kind of a leader?
   A. Autocratic   B. Democratic   C. Emergent   D. Informal

   1.____

2. Your boss is only effective as the leader of your department when you and your coworkers are motivated experts on the topic at hand. If any of you do not really have expertise in a given field, his leadership falters somewhat. What type of leader is your boss?
   A. Laissez-faire   B. Technical   C. Democratic   D. Autocratic

   2.____

3. If a leader is in charge of an inexperienced group that does not have the appropriate information and proficiency to successfully complete a task, which of the following approaches should the leader use in order for success to follow within the group?
   A. Yelling   B. Delegating   C. Participating   D. Selling

   3.____

4. If you are a democratic leader, which of the following styles will be reflective of your leadership technique?
   A. Participating   B. Telling   C. Yelling   D. Delegating

   4.____

5. In producing equality in group member participation, which of the following should a leader NOT do?
   A. Make a statement or ask a question after each person in the group has said something
   B. Avoid taking a position during disagreements
   C. Limit comments to specific individuals within the group
   D. Control dominating speakers

   5.____

6. Social capital is BEST defined as
   A. social connections that help us make more money
   B. social connections that improve our lives
   C. a type of connection that experts believe is becoming more common in Europe than the United States.
   D. none of the above

   6.____

7. Communication is not simply sending a message. It is creating true
   A. connectivity           B. understanding
   C. empathy               D. power

   7.____

29

8. Of the following, which is NOT a part of the speech communication process?   8._____
   A. Feedback              B. Central idea
   C. Interference          D. Ethics

9. You are leading a meeting and afterwards your colleagues tell you they didn't   9._____
   quite understand what you were communicating verbally and nonverbally to
   them. Which part of the communication process do you need to work on?
   A. Channel               B. Main idea
   C. Message               D. Specific purpose

10. If nonverbal messages contradict verbal symbols, you are sending what   10._____
    kind of message to your public?
    A. Clear                B. Mixed
    C. Controversial        D. Negative

11. Which of the following would a public speaker use to deliver verbal symbols?   11._____
    A. Words                B. Gestures
    C. Tone                 D. Facial expression

12. You are in the process of taking a course on interacting with the public. Your   12._____
    instructor starts talking about "the pathway" used to transmit a message. He
    explains that "the pathway" is better known as a
    A. link        B. loop        C. transmitter     D. channel

13. You finish an informational meeting with members of a community   13._____
    concerning a new park that will be built nearby. Afterwards, you are seeking
    feedback from them. Which of the following would NOT be a form of helpful
    feedback to you?
    A. Listeners raise their hands to point out a mistake
    B. Videotape the presentation
    C. Have colleagues and/or friends critique your presentation
    D. Hand out evaluation forms to listeners and have them fill it out after the
       presentation

14. Many public speaking experts have often repeated the famous quote, "A yawn   14._____
    is a silent _____," which references the quality of engagement within a
    presentation.
    A. rudeness    B. insult      C. shout          D. protest

15. If a child is running around during your speech and making a lot of noise,   15._____
    what type of interference would that be?
    A. Situational B. External    C. Internal       D. Intentional

16. According to multiple recent surveys, of the five biggest mistakes that   16._____
    speakers make during a presentation, which one is the WORST?
    A. Being poorly prepared
    B. Trying to cover too much in one speech
    C. Failing to tailor a speech to the needs and interests of the audience
    D. Being boring

17. One of your colleagues has been asked to lead a meeting, and she confides in you that she suffers from excessive stage fright. Which of the following areas should you advise her to focus on to prevent her fear?
    A. Preparation
    B. Self-confidence
    C. Experience
    D. Sense of humor

17.____

18. When interacting with the public, which of the following elements should you NEVER imagine before engaging in public speaking?
    A. Effective delivery
    B. Nervousness
    C. Possibility of failure
    D. Success

18.____

19. A spokesperson is giving a speech to community members and you are evaluating him. You notice he tends to focus too much on himself and not enough on his audience. What is one piece of advice you can give him so he can shift his focus more to his audience?
    A. Change his amount of eye contact
    B. Work on facial expressions
    C. Alter his style of speaking
    D. All of the above

19.____

20. Most experts agree that the best way to eliminate excess energy would be to do all of the following EXCEPT
    A. using visual aids
    B. gripping the lectern
    C. walking to the right and left occasionally
    D. making gestures

20.____

21. A woman has lived in Newville her whole life. Recently, the Newville public works department made a policy change that angered her since it completely rearranged her schedule. She calls you on the phone and displays her displeasure with your department's recent policy change. What is the FIRST response you should have toward her?
    A. Interrupt her to say you cannot discuss the situation until she calms down
    B. Apologize to her that she has been negatively affected by the public works department
    C. Listen to her and demonstrate comprehension of her situation and why she was upset by your department's action
    D. Give her a detailed explanation of the reasons for the policy change

21.____

22. Which of the following is generally TRUE regarding public opinion?
    A. It is hard to move people toward a strong opinion on anything
    B. It is easy to move people toward a strong opinion on anything
    C. Most public relations are devoted to repairing negative public opinion about individuals
    D. It is easier than previously thought to move people away from an opinion they hold

22.____

23. Influencing a community member's attitude really comes down to which of the following?
    A. Journalism
    B. Public relations
    C. Social psychology
    D. Social action groups

23.____

4 (#1)

24. If you attend a town hall meeting in which community members will bring up issues that require you to explain why your organization made the decisions it made, you will need to persuade them using evidence that is virtually indisputable. Which type of evidence should you stick to when explaining answers to the public?
    A. Facts
    B. Personal experience
    C. Emotions
    D. Using what appeals to the target public

25. In the last decade, especially after all the organizational and governmental scandals, public institutions must do which of the following in order to be successful?
    A. Work hard to earn and sustain favorable public opinion
    B. Trust the instincts expressed by the general public
    C. Be cognizant of the media's power
    D. Place the needs of the executives ahead of the needs of the public and other constituents

24.____

25.____

---

# KEY (CORRECT ANSWERS)

| | | | | |
|---|---|---|---|---|
| 1. | C | | 11. | A |
| 2. | A | | 12. | D |
| 3. | B | | 13. | A |
| 4. | D | | 14. | C |
| 5. | A | | 15. | B |
| 6. | B | | 16. | C |
| 7. | B | | 17. | A |
| 8. | D | | 18. | B |
| 9. | C | | 19. | D |
| 10. | B | | 20. | B |

21. C
22. D
23. B
24. A
25. A

---

# TEST 2

DIRECTIONS: Each question or incomplete statement is followed by several suggested answers or completions. Select the one that BEST answers the question or completes the statement. *PRINT THE LETTER OF THE CORRECT ANSWER IN THE SPACE AT THE RIGHT.*

1. Unique attributes of the Internet that people can enjoy include all of the following EXCEPT  1.____
    A. immediacy
    B. low cost
    C. pervasiveness
    D. value for building one-to-one human relationships

2. Which of the following is a reason that social media can be more effective than traditional means of advertising and communication?  2.____
    A. When someone mentions your brand in social media, there is much more potential for other people to notice
    B. It is easier to decipher tone and purpose through Twitter or Facebook than through personal communication
    C. Most of the people who would be interested in your brand or service are comfortable and familiar with using social media
    D. Almost anyone can step into a media relations role if primarily using social media, because it is easy to communicate effectively through social media platforms

3. You are tasked with building publicity for the upcoming reveal of a new art installation in the town you work in. Your boss tells you to contact journalists, reporters and bloggers to help spread the word. Which of the following would be the MOST effective way of getting the media to help build coverage?  3.____
    A. Send out a mass e-mail to any media members in the area detailing the art installation and why you need coverage for it
    B. Call each media outlet and find out who would most likely cover and build publicity for your project. Then reach out to them either face-to-face or through a phone call
    C. Using Twitter, tweet at the media members and introduce yourself and your art installation and ask them to help spread the word
    D. None of the above

4. When using written communication, which of the following is a MAJOR challenge of writing to listeners?  4.____
    A. Providing lots of statistics
    B. Grabbing the attention of the listener quickly
    C. Providing information that is easily reviewed
    D. Presenting lots of incidentals

5. In order to communicate well in writing, which of the following pieces of advice sounds good but doesn't actually help you?
   A. Write material for all audiences rather than focusing on one
   B. Think before writing
   C. Write simply and with clarity
   D. Write and rewrite until you have a polished, finished product

6. You send out a public newsletter that details a project that your team is currently working on. One week later, an employee on your team tells you she has received multiple phone calls from confused constituents claiming that the newsletter's readability was low. When you send out a corrected newsletter, you need to make sure that your communication is easy to
   A. read   B. hear   C. edit   D. comprehend

7. You work for a biomedical company as a public outreach advocate. One day, an exciting e-mail circulates internally that states one of your scientists has discovered a cure for leukemia and your supervisor tasks you with writing the release. When writing the release, the newsworthy element inherent in the story is
   A. oddity   B. conflict   C. impact   D. proximity

8. When communicating with the public through the Internet, news releases
   A. should not be sent via e-mail
   B. should be succinct
   C. should be sent via "snail mail"
   D. none of the above

9. What is the MAJOR advantage of organizational publications?
   Their ability to
   A. give sponsoring organizations a means of uncontrolled communications
   B. deliver specific, detailed information to narrowly defined target publics
   C. avoid the problems typically associated with two-way media
   D. provide a revenue source for sponsoring organizations

10. You are confronted by a question from a reporter that you do not know the answer to. What should you do?
    A. Give them other information you are certain is right
    B. Tell them that information is "off the record" and will be distributed later
    C. Say "no comment" rather than look like you're uninformed
    D. Admit that you don't know but promise to provide the information later

11. Often times, an organization will run situation analysis before they share information with the public. Which one of these "internal factors" is usually associated with a situational analysis?
    A. A communication audit
    B. Community focus groups
    C. A list of media contacts
    D. Strategy suggestions

12. When you are hired, your first task is to start a process of identifying who are involved and affected by a situation central to your organization. This process is MOST commonly referred to as a(n)
    A. situation interview
    B. communication audit
    C. exploratory survey
    D. stakeholder analysis

13. Once a public outreach plan is in the summative evaluation phase, which of the following is generally associated with it?
    A. Impact
    B. Implementation
    C. Attitude change
    D. Preparation

14. Which of the following Internet-related challenges is MOST significant in the public relations field?
    A. Finding stable, cost-effective internet provides
    B. Representing clients using new social media environments
    C. Staying abreast of changing technology
    D. Training staff to use social media

15. Which of the following BEST defines a public issue? Any
    A. problem that brings a public lawsuit
    B. concern that is of mutual distress to competitors
    C. issue that is of mutual concern to an organization and its stakeholders
    D. problem that is not a concern to an organization and/or one of its stakeholders

16. A handful of people are posting misleading and/or negative information about your organization. What is the MOST proactive approach to handling this situation?
    A. Buy up enough shares in the site where the negative posts are, and prevent those users from posting again
    B. Post anonymous comments on the sites to help combat the negativity
    C. Prepare news releases that discredit the inaccuracies
    D. Make policy changes to address complaints highlighted on the sites

17. Your supervisor has recently asked you to review present and future realities for interacting with the public. Why is it important to continually review these?
    A. It helps develop your vision statement
    B. It helps interpret trends for management
    C. It helps construe the organization's business plan
    D. To know what path the company should pursue

18. You are the community relations director for the public water utility plant that has been the focus of a group of activists who are opposed to the addition of fluoride to drinking water. These objectors are not only at the plant each day, but they are also very active on social media inciting negativity towards the practice. As the director of the plant, you have overwhelming evidence that contradicts what the protestors are arguing. You want to combat their social media with your own internet plan. Which of the following is the MOST appropriate action for you to take?
    A. Use utility employees to write the blog, posing as healthcare professionals
    B. Reach out to medical professionals to volunteer to tweet and message community members under their own identities, but with no reference to the utility company
    C. Write a blog yourself, identifying yourself as an employee, and quote the scientific opinions of a variety of sources
    D. Pay for medical professionals to respond through the internet, identifying the utility as their sponsor, but without disclosing the compensation

18.____

19. You have recently completed an advertising campaign to help assuage the anger of the community at changes in the upcoming summer program for the city. Which of the following measurements would be MOST effective for evaluating the campaign's impact on audience attitude?
    A. A content analysis of media coverage
    B. Studying blog postings about the issue
    C. Analyzing pre- and post-numbers of people signed up for the summer programs
    D. Conducting a pre- and post-analysis of public opinions

19.____

20. In order to measure how policy changes will affect the public, you recommend that your supervisors first run a focus group for research. They like the idea, but want you to be in charge of running the group. Which of the following should you keep in mind as you form the focus group?
    A. Participants need to be randomly selected
    B. Make sure participants are radically different from one another so you get a range of opinions
    C. Include at least seven or more people in the group. Otherwise, the sample is too small to draw any conclusions.
    D. Formulate a research plan and use it as a script so you can make sure the results are ones that will work for you and your supervisors

20.____

21. The public university has recently come under fire for not offering enough tuition savings options for students. You have been hired to help promote the programs they offer including new savings programs. What is the MOST appropriate first step for you to take?
    A. Research pricing and development costs for the services
    B. Develop a survey to discover which factors impact families' savings
    C. Conduct a situation analysis to gain better understanding of the issues
    D. Hold a focus group to determine which messages would be most effective for your program

21.____

22. After receiving feedback from the public on a new program, you are concerned the results have been tainted by courtesy bias. You plan on sending out a new questionnaire, but you need to make sure the bias is discouraged in it. Which of the following techniques will be MOST effective at decreasing the partiality?
    A. Make questionnaire responses confidential
    B. Employ an outside firm to run the survey
    C. Offer a larger range of responses in the survey
    D. Both "A" and "C"

22.____

23. You have just relocated from Omaha, Nebraska to a branch in Chicago, Illinois. In order to communicate well while in Chicago, you must remember that
    A. most publics have the same needs
    B. all publics are most interested only in technology you are using
    C. each audience has its own special needs and require different types of communication
    D. all audiences' needs overlap

23.____

24. Recently, the Parks and Recreation Department has come under fire because it has been accused of too much marketing and not enough public relations. Which of the following, if true, would lend credibility to these accusations?
    A. Employees are focused on signing citizens up for as many different camps and activities available over the summer as possible
    B. Management consistently tries to send appreciation gifts to members of the community when they have volunteered or attending an activity sponsored by the Park district
    C. Weekly meetings are held to determine how to best improve the Park district's image as it relates to consumers
    D. Parks and Recreation is primarily focused on making sure the public enjoys their activities and trusts them to put on educational programs for the children

24.____

25. During your speech, a community member stands up and accuses you of "spinning" a story. Which of the following BEST describes their accusation?
    A. You are relating a message through an agreed-upon ethical practice within the public relations community
    B. You are twisting a message to create performance where there is none
    C. You are trying to preserve hard-earned credibility
    D. You are providing the media with balanced and accurate information

25.____

## KEY (CORRECT ANSWERS)

| | | | |
|---|---|---|---|
| 1. | D | 11. | A |
| 2. | A | 12. | D |
| 3. | C | 13. | A |
| 4. | B | 14. | C |
| 5. | D | 15. | C |
| 6. | D | 16. | B |
| 7. | C | 17. | A |
| 8. | B | 18. | C |
| 9. | B | 19. | D |
| 10. | D | 20. | A |

21. C
22. D
23. C
24. A
25. B

# TEST 3

DIRECTIONS: Each question or incomplete statement is followed by several suggested answers or completions. Select the one that BEST answers the question or completes the statement. *PRINT THE LETTER OF THE CORRECT ANSWER IN THE SPACE AT THE RIGHT.*

1. In order to be successful in relating to the public, all of the following are vital EXCEPT
   A. performance
   B. relationship building
   C. formal education
   D. diversity of experience

   1.____

2. Which of the following is TRUE of communicating well regarding public relations experts?
   A. It will differentiate you and your role from others with special skills in the organization you work for
   B. It should be handled delicately in order to avoid upsetting stakeholders
   C. It is not as important as looking fashionable
   D. It is less important than understanding bureaucratic peculiarities

   2.____

3. You are critiquing a staffer who will lead an important meeting in two days and you note that she keeps using words that are steeped with connotation. You tell her to be careful of these words. Why?
   A. They transmit meaning too clearly, and you always want to leave wiggle room in your meaning
   B. They transmit the dictionary definition of a word that makes for a boring presentation
   C. They transmit meaning with an emotional overtone that could lead to misunderstanding in an overall message
   D. They lend themselves to stereotyping

   3.____

4. If you are trying to avoid biasing your intended audience, which of the following factors could help with that?
   A. Symbols
   B. Objective reporting by media
   C. Semantics
   D. Peers

   4.____

5. Of the following, which trait is MOST desirable when working with the public?
   A. Having the "gift for gab"
   B. Being an elite strategist
   C. Being able to leap organizational boundaries
   D. Performing well, especially in crises

   5.____

6. Which of the following areas is likely to see continual growth in the practice of public relations?
   A. Healthcare
   B. Social media
   C. Law enforcement
   D. None of the above

   6.____

7. What is the MOST commonly used public relations tactic?
   A. A news release
   B. A special event
   C. A PSA (public service announcement)
   D. A full feature news article

7.____

8. You have just been assigned to help with a new advertising campaign that will promote the new services offered by your organization. One major component of the new campaign will focus on publicity through photographs. Knowing you need to get this part of the project right, which of the following is the BEST tip to remember when taking PR photos?
   A. Don't use action shots because they usually wind up blurry
   B. Make sure there is good contrast and sharp detail
   C. Ensure that the product/services are the biggest thing(s) in the photo
   D. Photograph multiple people rather than only one

8.____

9. Which of the following situations would merit holding a press conference?
   A. When a corporation is restructured
   B. When a new public relations employee has been hired
   C. When information is of minor relevance to a specific audience
   D. When there is a new product to be released

9.____

10. On average, how long should an announcement to the public last on the radio?
    A. 2 minutes    B. 20 seconds    C. 1 minute    D. 10 seconds

10.____

11. In educating the public, you need to develop a PR plan and analyze each situation that could arise. Which of the following should NOT be a part of the analysis?
    A. Research                         B. Message crafting
    C. Creating a problem statement     D. Asking the 5 W's and the H

11.____

12. You are in charge of promoting an event in the near future, but social media is unavailable to you at this time. Which of the following is the BEST way to get your message out to the media and, therefore, the public?
    A. An Op-Ed piece in the local newspaper
    B. A press conference
    C. A newsletter
    D. A news release

12.____

13. In the past few months, you and your colleagues have been accused of "doublespeak". Which of the following excerpts from presentations you have used could you defend and explain why it would NOT be an example of "doublespeak"?
    A. You called combat "fighting"
    B. Fred referred to genocide as "ethnic cleansing"
    C. Your boss referred to recent layoffs as "downsizing"
    D. Susie called the janitor a "custodial engineer"

13.____

14. In relating to the public, which of the following reflects key words in defining modern day PR?
    A. Deliberate, public interest, management function
    B. Persuasive, manipulative, improvisation
    C. Management, technical, flexible
    D. Influential, creative, evaluative

15. How is educating and relating to the public different from being a journalist, marketing agent, or advertiser?
    A. It is more focused on advocacy
    B. It is about getting "free" press coverage
    C. It is about building relationships with various demographics
    D. All of the above

16. Of the following, what is the BEST tactic for learning employee attitudes?
    A. Internal communications audit    B. Research
    C. Conference meeting               D. Both A and B

17. When releasing news to the public, you should make sure it reads at a _____-grade reading level.
    A. 5th        B. 12th        C. 9th        D. 7th

18. If you are using a euphemism that actually changes the meaning/impact of a concept you are trying to relay, what is that called?
    A. Insider language       B. Doublespeak
    C. Stylizing              D. Plagiarism

19. Which of the following should be included in a public relations campaign if you want to ensure people will hear, understand, and believe your message?
    A. Repetition             B. Imagery
    C. Thoroughness           D. Acceptance

20. In PR, what is it called when you track coverage and compare it over a period of time?
    A. Bookmarking            B. Benchmarking
    C. Comparison analysis    D. Correspondence

21. What is a baseline study PRIMARILY used for?
    A. To determine changes in audience perception and attitude
    B. To figure out how well your company is doing in the marketplace compared to your competitors
    C. To find out the cost of buying space taken up by a particular article if that article is an advertisement
    D. None of the above

22. Of the following people, who would BEST be considered a modern role model for successful public relations?
    A. Phineas T. Barnum (Barnum and Bailey)
    B. Ivy Lee
    C. Andrew Jackson
    D. Sir Walter Raleigh

22.____

23. If your organization has recently participated in a "publicity stunt," what type of PR strategy have you just used?
    A. Community
    B. Lobbying
    C. News management
    D. Crisis management

23.____

24. You tell your supervisor that you want to start using video press releases. When he presses you to explain why, you tell him that you want to take advantage of the fact that
    A. many news agencies don't review them ahead of broadcasting
    B. most reporters hired to create them have contacts within the industry
    C. they cover stories that some local news organizations cannot
    D. the production value may be better than those at local stations

24.____

25. A _____ is a type of news leak in which the source reveals large policy changes are on the table.
    A. disclosure    B. hook    C. exclusive    D. trial balloon

25.____

## KEY (CORRECT ANSWERS)

1. C
2. B
3. C
4. B
5. D

6. B
7. A
8. B
9. D
10. C

11. B
12. D
13. A
14. A
15. D

16. D
17. C
18. B
19. A
20. B

21. A
22. B
23. C
24. C
25. D

# TEST 4

DIRECTIONS: Each question or incomplete statement is followed by several suggested answers or completions. Select the one that BEST answers the question or completes the statement. *PRINT THE LETTER OF THE CORRECT ANSWER IN THE SPACE AT THE RIGHT.*

1. The Facial Feedback Hypothesis is a popular nonverbal theory that is BEST defined as
    A. people mirroring each other's facial expressions
    B. emotions leading to certain facial expressions
    C. facial expression can lead to the experience of certain emotions
    D. looking into a mirror while making a facial expression can cause one to change their facial expression

2. Of the following, which is NOT recognized as a function of smiling?
    A. It provides feedback.
    B. It signals disinterest.
    C. It helps establish rapport.
    D. It signals attentiveness.

3. When facial expressions are limited by cultural expectations, that is referred to as
    A. display rules
    B. syntactic displays
    C. adaptors
    D. interaction intensification

4. Of the following, which is recognized as part of the six basic emotions across cultures globally?
    A. Guilt
    B. Happiness
    C. Fear
    D. Both B and C

5. Which kinds of communication scenarios are more likely to see leadership roles develop from?
    A. Small group
    B. Intrapersonal communication
    C. Face-to-face public communication
    D. Text messaging

6. Which of the following highlights the key difference between small group communication and organizational communication?
    A. Feedback is easier and more immediate in organizational.
    B. Communication is more informal in small group communication.
    C. The message is easier to adapt to the specific needs of the receiver in organizational communication.
    D. People are more spread out in small group communication.

7. Which of the following would be an example of mediated communication?
    A. A principal addresses the student body in a speech.
    B. Two friends communicate while they work together in class.
    C. An employee texts his coworkers to see if they want to hang out after work.
    D. Three friends joke with one another while attending a concert.

8. Which of the following is FALSE concerning the way interpersonal relationships can affect us physically?
    A. Without interpersonal relationships, we can become sick
    B. These interpersonal relationships are necessary for humans; according to most research, humans raised in isolation are less healthy than those raised with others
    C. Humans are not the only mammals that need relationships in order to survive and thrive
    D. Interpersonal relationships are necessary until about age 12, but not later in adulthood

9. Which of the following is a characteristic of public relationships as they compare to private relationships?
    A. Intrinsic rewards
    B. Normative rules
    C. Use of particularistic knowledge
    D. Small number of intimates

10. When someone asks how you know they were angry, it is likely they fall into which style of facial expressions?
    A. Withholder
    B. Revealer
    C. Frozen-affect expressor
    D. Unwitting expressor

11. The theory of expectancy violations is BEST defined as
    A. nonverbal behavior reciprocated based primarily on positive or negative valence and the perceived reward value of the other person
    B. the process of intimacy exchange within a dyad relationship
    C. a social rule that says we should repay in kind what another has provided us
    D. none of the above

12. If an employee has a very good idea of what is and is not socially acceptable in any given situation, which kind of linguistic competence is she strong in?
    A. Phonemic    B. Syntactic    C. Pragmatic    D. Semantic

13. Which of the following would NOT be considered sexist language?
    A. Although a girl, Sonia is very brave.
    B. A gorgeous model, Johnny also likes to use his surfboard on the weekends.
    C. Jimmy's brother is a male nurse.
    D. None; all are considered to be sexist.

14. What is it called when individual experience, and NOT conventional agreement, creates meaning?
    A. Small talk communication
    B. Denotative meaning
    C. Connotative meaning
    D. Self-reflexive communication

15. Which of the following kinds of communication do students spend the MOST time engaged in?
    A. Listening    B. Writing    C. Reading    D. Speaking

16. Which of the following would be evidence of active listening?  16.____
    A. Maintain eye contact      B. Nodding and making eye contact
    C. Asking for clarification  D. All of the above

17. When listening in an evaluative context, which of the following must be done  17.____
    for it to be considered successful?
    A. Precisely disseminate stimuli in a message
    B. Comprehend the intended meaning of a message
    C. Make critical assessments of the accuracy of the facts in a message
    D. All of the above

18. A friend visits one day and tells you she thinks her husband is cheating on her  18.____
    with his ex-wife. She tells you she doesn't know what to do because she can't
    imagine living without him. If you wanted to paraphrase, which of the following
    BEST exemplifies that?
    A. "You are feeling insecure because you don't have a very good
       relationship with your husband."
    B. "You're afraid your husband is seeing his ex-wife behind your back; you
       don't know what to do; and you can't live without him."
    C. "You're afraid that your husband may still have feelings for his ex-wife and
       you're afraid you'll lose him."
    D. "Don't worry; his ex-wife is not back with him. You're just being paranoid."

19. When we form impressions of others, when might the recency effect impact  19.____
    our assessments? If we
    A. focus on our own feelings instead of the feelings of others
    B. are motivated to be more accurate or expect to be held accountable for
       our own perceptions
    C. engage in self-monitoring of our behaviors
    D. employ the discounting rule

20. Which of the following BEST defines a "modal self"?  20.____
    A. The ideal person for a social order
    B. A person who does not go to extremes
    C. The kind of self valued in the 20$^{th}$ century but not the 21$^{st}$ century
    D. The person who monitors his own behavior in social situations

21. Which of the following is TRUE of today's society?  21.____
    A. People are less selfish than they have ever been.
    B. People spend most of their time trying to be a single, unitary self.
    C. People have many short-lived relationships leading to their notions of
       themselves changing easily.
    D. People try to be frugal, honorable, and self-sacrificing.

22. A man's childhood consisted of a dismissing attachment style. Which of the following behaviors will he MOST likely exhibit as an adult?
    A. Anxiousness and ambivalence
    B. Obsessive friendliness and dependence
    C. Autonomy and distance from others
    D. Rhetorical sensitivity

22._____

23. When practicing self-disclosure, which of the following is a good rule of thumb?
    A. Be sure to disclose more than your partner
    B. Reserve your most important disclosures for people you know well
    C. Ignore the style of disclosure; the only thing that is important is content
    D. All of the above

23._____

24. During your first meeting as project leader, you approach your group and inform them that John will serve as your assistant project leader. He will be responsible for chairing team meetings and establishing the agenda. When John is given this formal leadership position, what type of power does he have over the other members of the project?
    A. Legitimate      B. Reward      C. Expert      D. Punishment

24._____

25. If you bring an employee to lead a project because she is knowledgeable and skilled in the area the project focuses on, what type of power does she possess?
    A. Legitimate      B. Reward      C. Referent      D. Expert

25._____

## KEY (CORRECT ANSWERS)

| | | | | |
|---|---|---|---|---|
| 1. | C | | 11. | A |
| 2. | B | | 12. | C |
| 3. | A | | 13. | D |
| 4. | D | | 14. | C |
| 5. | A | | 15. | A |
| 6. | B | | 16. | D |
| 7. | C | | 17. | C |
| 8. | D | | 18. | B |
| 9. | B | | 19. | D |
| 10. | D | | 20. | A |

21. C
22. C
23. B
24. A
25. D

# EXAMINATION SECTION
# TEST 1

DIRECTIONS: Each question or incomplete statement is followed by several suggested answers or completions. Select the one that BEST answers the question or completes the statement. *PRINT THE LETTER OF THE CORRECT ANSWER IN THE SPACE AT THE RIGHT.*

1. Which of the following is NOT essential information that you need to know about your audience?  1.____
    A. How big the audience is
    B. What the audience is interested in
    C. What type of mood the audience is in
    D. If their attendance was mandatory or not

2. Which of the following is NOT one of the main reasons to communicate with the masses?  2.____
    A. Surveillance
    B. Entertainment
    C. Cultural transmission
    D. Correlation

3. Which of the following is true regarding e-mail?  3.____
    A. E-mail changes only the message
    B. E-mail changes only the way the message is delivered
    C. E-mail changes the way the message is delivered and the message itself
    D. E-mail changes neither the way the message is delivered nor the message itself

4. The best way to promote effective communication is  4.____
    A. practice good learning skills
    B. be aware of body language
    C. maintain eye contact
    D. all of the above

5. Before starting a speech, what should every public speaker make sure to do?  5.____
    A. Read through their notes really quickly
    B. Visualize their success in giving the speech
    C. Drink a lot of water so they are hydrated
    D. None of the above

6. The most important goal of business communication is  6.____
    A. a favorable relationship between speaker and listener
    B. administrative cohesion
    C. listener response
    D. listener understanding

7. Which of the following is an example of external communication?  7._____
   A. Meeting of employees in the purchasing department
   B. Telephone call from the area manager to the branch manager
   C. Letter from a supplier
   D. Discussion between a manager and an assistant

8. When introducing someone to an audience, which of the following should you avoid mentioning?  8._____
   A. Honors/accolades they received
   B. Recent or significant educational accomplishments
   C. Humor or jokes to lighten up the crowd
   D. Media attention or publications

9. Your office has organized a series of public events to prepare residents for the coming hurricane season. It is your job to inform attendees about the proper precautions to take when securing their homes and protecting their belongings in the event of a major storm. The BEST way to do this is to  9._____
   A. hand out detailed brochures and answer questions while experts demonstrate appropriate methods and procedures
   B. distribute brochures as well as pamphlets with information on how to view demonstrations on your office's YouTube channel
   C. give out magnets and paperweights containing a URL link to a storm-preparation website
   D. hand out storm-readiness pamphlets at the entrance along with a voucher for a free popcorn and soda

10. Which of the following would NOT be considered part of project management?  10._____
    A. A clearly stated objective
    B. A timeline for beginning and ending the project
    C. Complex tasks and/or intricate teamwork
    D. None of the above

11. What is the best way to recognize an employee who has gone above and beyond their job expectations?  11._____
    A. Celebrate his success with the whole team or group
    B. Take him out to a one-on-one lunch and tell him how special he is
    C. Ask him what sort of extra benefit or reward he would like for doing such a great job
    D. Give him a "Thank You" card signed by his coworkers

12. Your friend has been supervising a group of people for the last 18 months. He tells you that in this time, none of his employees reported any problems to him. He asks you if you think this is a problem. You should tell him
    A. he is doing great and there is no room for improvement
    B. his staff is relatively small, so the chance of problems arising are smaller than if he had a larger group
    C. his staff may be reluctant to discuss problems with him so he should ask them if there are any concerns
    D. his employees are competent and are handling their problems well by themselves.

12.\_\_\_\_\_

13. Which of the following BEST describes a physiological noise?
    A. Weed whacker
    B. Air conditioner
    C. Listener reviewing their to-do list while you're speaking
    D. A speaker using complex terms

13.\_\_\_\_\_

14. The ability to feel compassion and understanding for another person's situation is
    A. empathy
    B. common sense
    C. professionalism
    D. audience analysis

14.\_\_\_\_\_

15. A longtime employee suddenly starts coming in late to work a couple of times each week. What is the best approach to solve this problem?
    A. Tell coworkers to talk to the employee to see what is going on
    B. Meet with the employee to tell her she needs to stop coming in late
    C. Dock her pay and tell her if it doesn't stop she will be fired
    D. All of the above

15.\_\_\_\_\_

16. You are in a meeting with your boss and a representative from a company that your team does business with. During the meeting, the representative hands you and your supervisor an expensive watch, which your boss eagerly accepts. What should you do?
    A. Accept the gift – your boss approves
    B. Refuse the gift – your supervisor's acceptance does not mean the company approves of the gift
    C. Accept the gift and then give it to a friend later – this way you don't make a scene
    D. Accept the gift as long as the representative knows that it won't give him any preferential treatment

16.\_\_\_\_\_

17. In the interviews for a vacant clerical position, none of the job candidates have all the skills necessary to do the job competently. Which candidate would be the BEST option for your company?
    A. Marianne, who has no formal education and says she can do the job based on her related work experience
    B. Jason, who has no related experience but lots of enthusiasm to learn to do the job
    C. Gillian, who has completed a related training program but has no experience
    D. None of the above – re-advertise and find more qualified help

17._____

18. Which of the following would benefit the most from strong project management?
    A. Processing an insurance claim
    B. Making an automobile
    C. Writing an essay
    D. Finishing a college degree

18._____

19. During the _____ stage, objectives are stated, the team is put together, and responsibilities are assigned.
    A. conceptualization
    B. definition
    C. planning
    D. execution

19._____

20. Which of the following is the most widely used source of information about events currently happening in the world?
    A. TV
    B. Radio
    C. Newspapers
    D. Professional journals

20._____

21. A customer complained to your supervisor because during a conversation about water conservation, you said it was "idiotic" for people to let hoses run when not in use. A more acceptable term would have been
    A. reckless
    B. moronic
    C. irresponsible
    D. mind-boggling

21._____

22. Your supervisor reprimands a worker for his neglect of duty, but he does it in a very public and embarrassing way. Which of the following would have been the best action for your supervisor to take?
    A. Tell the employee about the neglect but in a private meeting
    B. Tell the employee about his good points and downplay the bad in private
    C. Allow the employee to begin with a clean record by avoiding criticism
    D. Nothing was wrong with how your supervisor handled the situation

22._____

23. Verbal and nonverbal responses to a message are called 23._____
    A. nonverbal code
    B. verbal code
    C. feedback
    D. external interference

24. One of your coworkers is involved in an increasingly animated conversation with a client. You intervene, and the coworker says he's trying to explain a company policy and doesn't appreciate the client's dismissive body language. Which of the following actions by the client might be the cause of the tension? 24._____
    A. Constant interrupting during the explanation
    B. Lack of eye contact
    C. A derisive sneer or hand gesture when he doesn't like the explanation
    D. Evading questions

25. You are in a customer service job and someone with a speech impairment has called you. What is the most effective way to communicate with them? 25._____
    A. Repeat his answer back to his to make sure you understood what he said
    B. Give him as much time as he needs to finish his statements
    C. Try to finish his sentences if he seems to struggle
    D. Try to make the conversation as short as possible so it won't be awkward

---

## KEY (CORRECT ANSWERS)

| | | |
|---|---|---|
| 1. D | 11. A | 21. C |
| 2. A | 12. C | 22. A |
| 3. B | 13. C | 23. C |
| 4. D | 14. A | 24. C |
| 5. B | 15. B | 25. B |
| 6. A | 16. B | |
| 7. C | 17. D | |
| 8. C | 18. B | |
| 9. A | 19. C | |
| 10. D | 20. A | |

# TEST 2

DIRECTIONS: Each question or incomplete statement is followed by several suggested answers or completions. Select the one that BEST answers the question or completes the statement. *PRINT THE LETTER OF THE CORRECT ANSWER IN THE SPACE AT THE RIGHT.*

1. If you are interacting with a customer who is not speaking, which of the following would be considered negative body language that they are sending to you?
    A. Facing you while you're talking
    B. If they roll their eyes at you
    C. If they are sitting in a relaxed position
    D. If they maintain eye contact

1._____

2. Which of the following is NOT a barrier to communicating in an effective manner?
    A. Interrupting someone who is speaking to you
    B. Complaining too much while speaking to a coworker
    C. Obscuring your face with your hand or a piece of paper
    D. Making a broad opening statement

2._____

3. A client requests a photo of a recent meeting. Which of the following types of files would you NOT send?
    A. .jpg
    B. .tif
    C. .png
    D. .mov

3._____

4. Although accuracy and speed are both vital in work performance, accuracy is more important because
    A. most supervisors insist on accurate work
    B. too much time is lost in correcting errors
    C. rapid work rates cannot be maintained for any real length of time
    D. speedy workers are too inaccurate

4._____

5. You recently gave an interview to a local television news reporter about measures the town government is taking to improve playground safety. Community feedback has been almost entirely negative.
What is a likely reason for this type of feedback?
    A. Important information was left out in favor of promotion of unrelated town programs and events
    B. Delivery of information was slow and measured
    C. The reporter's questions were very direct
    D. The safety program is a waste of taxpayer money

5._____

6. Your department was responsible for a local barbecue and volleyball tournament that raised more than $10,000 for cancer research. Feedback from attendees and local businesses was overwhelmingly positive, and many stated their interest in participating again next year. However, in the comments section associated with an Internet newspaper article about the event, several anonymous users said the event was a waste of money, the food was terrible and the volleyball referees were biased. Some users also made derogatory statements about people in the event photos.
As one of the organizers of the event, you should

    A. ignore the comments – direct feedback from the community was positive, and the opinions of anonymous commenters have no value
    B. have the newspaper publish a full-page ad thanking the community for its support
    C. demand that the newspaper remove negative commentary as it might hurt the success of next year's event
    D. respond directly to the commenters to help them understand the importance of the fundraiser

6.\_\_\_\_\_

7. What is implied by the statement, "Communication is a process"?
    A. There is a clear beginning and end point to it
    B. Communication more closely resembles a photo rather than a movie
    C. Communication is continuous and ongoing
    D. None of the above

7.\_\_\_\_\_

8. You need your employees to work overtime. Which of the following would be the best way to break the news?
    A. Tell them you'd consider it a personal favor for them to work overtime
    B. Tell them why the overtime is necessary
    C. Reassure them that they can take time off in the future
    D. Remind them that working overtime is part of their job description

8.\_\_\_\_\_

9. A specific behavior may be acceptable in one situation and inappropriate in another. This example best illustrates the idea that communication aptitude
    A. includes choosing poor behaviors
    B. includes being combative
    C. includes being extremely intelligent
    D. is situational

9.\_\_\_\_\_

10. You are training at your new job and you spend today learning about the forms and paperwork used by the company in customer relations. What area of training would this fall under?
    A. Interpersonal skills
    B. Customer knowledge
    C. Technical skills
    D. Product and service knowledge

10.\_\_\_\_\_

11. If you need to revise and edit a document for your boss, you should  11._____
    A. spell and grammar check on the computer
    B. read the draft out loud
    C. quick-read the draft.
    D. analyze the draft in one reading

12. Which of the following is an example of self-monitoring?  12._____
    A. Having a checklist to refer to for skills to practice
    B. Listening to your own voice while speaking with others
    C. Watching others react to your jokes
    D. All of the above

13. A tractor driving by and interfering with your conversation is an example of what kind of noise?  13._____
    A. External
    B. Psychological
    C. Psychological
    D. Internal

14. It is casual Friday and your boss disapproves of the music group pictured on your shirt. His attitude toward you in your staff meeting is frosty and distant. This is an example of what kind of communication distraction?  14._____
    A. External
    B. Psychological
    C. Physiological
    D. Internal

15. In the majority of situations, proficient communicators can  15._____
    A. choose from a wide variety of behaviors
    B. demonstrate empathy
    C. use self-monitoring to improve their communication skills
    D. all of the above

16. Mass communication usually tends to be  16._____
    A. one way
    B. communication from one to many
    C. anonymous
    D. none of the above

17. When communicating, to encode a message means  17._____
    A. speaking to large groups of people
    B. blocking a pathway between the sender and receiver of a message
    C. translate an idea into coded message
    D. interpret a coded message

18. Which of the following is a way to provide feedback when communicating?  18._____
    A. Verbally
    B. Nonverbally
    C. Through environmental noise
    D. Verbally and nonverbally from the listener

19. When creating a vacation schedule for your employees, which of the following is least important to consider?  19._____
    A. Employee proficiency
    B. Employee preference
    C. Anticipated workload for each quarter
    D. How pertinent each employee's services are during each vacation period

20. When thinking about the range and scope of an e-mail, you should consider  20._____
    A. the amount of detail needed in the message
    B. how technical the document should be
    C. what format the audience expects
    D. all of the above

21. You discover that one of your colleagues has received bribes from a business to make sure their bid for a project is accepted. What should you do?  21._____
    A. Pretend that you didn't hear anything and do nothing
    B. Report it to management
    C. Ask your colleague to stop his unethical behavior
    D. Ask your manager to be transferred to a different department

22. If the person you are talking to has a hearing problem that is causing a communication barrier between the two of you, what should you do to help overcome this barrier?  22._____
    A. Find someone who knows sign language
    B. Learn sign language yourself
    C. Speak louder or put your message in writing
    D. Suggest to the person that they need to get medical attention

23. When a supervisor assigns work to his team members, which of the following criteria would be the best for them to use?  23._____
    A. Allow each employee to choose which tasks he or she is the best at
    B. Assign the more difficult work to newer team members
    C. Give any tedious/unimportant work to slower employees
    D. Delegate assignments based on the abilities of employees

24. Which of the following is true of writing skills for a professional in the workplace?  24._____
    A. They are rarely used because the Internet makes writing unnecessary
    B. They are not required because secretaries do most of the writing for professionals
    C. They are important but not essential because many pre-designed templates are available to use
    D. They are a key job requirement and are frequently listed in professional job descriptions

25. The method of writers working together to create memos, letters or other business documents is called _____ writing.
    A. choreographed
    B. combative
    C. collaborative
    D. coalesced

25._____

---

## KEY (CORRECT ANSWERS)

| | | |
|---|---|---|
| 1. B | 11. B | 21. B |
| 2. D | 12. D | 22. A |
| 3. D | 13. A | 23. D |
| 4. A | 14. B | 24. D |
| 5. A | 15. D | 25. C |
| | | |
| 6. A | 16. B | |
| 7. C | 17. C | |
| 8. C | 18. D | |
| 9. D | 19. A | |
| 10. C | 20. D | |

---

# EXAMINATION SECTION
# TEST 1

DIRECTIONS: Each question or incomplete statement is followed by several suggested answers or completions. Select the one that BEST answers the question or completes the statement. *PRINT THE LETTER OF THE CORRECT ANSWER IN THE SPACE AT THE RIGHT.*

1. Good procedure in handling complaints from the public may be divided into the following four principal stages:
   I. Investigation of the complaint
   II. Receipt of the complaint
   III. Assignment of responsibility for investigation and correction
   IV. Notification of correction

   The ORDER in which these stages ordinarily come is:
   A. III, II, I, IV
   B. II, III, I, IV
   C. II, III, IV, I
   D. II, IV, III, I

   1.____

2. The department may expect the MOST severe public criticism if
   A. it asks for an increase in its annual budget
   B. it purchases new and costly street cleaning equipment
   C. sanitation officers and men are reclassified to higher salary grades
   D. there is delay in cleaning streets of snow

   2.____

3. The MOST important function of public relations in the department should be to
   A. develop cooperation on the part of the public in keeping streets clean
   B. get stricter penalties enacted for health code violations
   C. recruit candidates for entrance positions who ca be developed into supervisors
   D. train career personnel so that they can advance in the department

   3.____

4. The one of the following which has MOST frequently elicited unfavorable public comment has been
   A. dirty sidewalks or streets
   B. dumping on lot
   C. failure to curb dogs
   D. overflowing garbage cans

   4.____

5. It has been suggested that, as a public relations measure, sections hold *open house* for the public.
   The MOST effective time for this would be
   A. during the summer when children are not in school and can accompany their parents
   B. during the winter when show is likely to fall and the public can see snow removal preparations
   C. immediately after a heavy snow storm when department snow removal operations are in full progress
   D. when street sanitation is receiving general attention as during *Keep City Clean* week

   5.____

6. When a public agency conducts a public relations program, it is MOST likely to find that each recipient of its message will
   A. disagree with the basic purpose of the message if the officials are not well known to him
   B. accept the message if it is presented by someone perceived as having a definite intention to persuade
   C. ignore the message unless it is presented in a literate and clever manner
   D. give greater attention to certain portions of the message as a result of his individual and cultural differences

7. Following are three statements about public relations and communications:
   I. A person who seeks to influence public opinion can speed up a trend
   II. Mass communications is the exposure of a mass audience to an idea
   III. All media are equally effective in reaching opinion leaders
   Which of the following choices CORRECTLY classifies the above statements into those which are correct and those which are not?
   A. I and II are correct, but III is not.
   B. II and III are correct, but I is not.
   C. I and III are correct, but II is not.
   D. III is correct, but I and II are not.

8. Public relations experts say that MAXIMUM effect for a message results from
   A. concentrating in one medium
   B. ignoring mass media and concentrating on *opinion makers*
   C. presenting only those factors which support a given position
   D. using a combination of two or more of the available media

9. To assure credibility and avoid hostility, the public relations man MUST
   A. make certain his message is truthful, not evasive or exaggerated
   B. make sure his message contains some dire consequence if ignored
   C. repeat the message often enough so that it cannot be ignored
   D. try to reach as many people and groups as possible

10. The public relations man MUST be prepared to assume that members of his audience
    A. may have developed attitudes toward his proposals—favorable, neutral, or unfavorable
    B. will be immediately hostile
    C. will consider his proposals with an open mind
    D. will invariably need an introduction to his subject

11. The one of the following statements that is CORRECT is:
    A. When a stupid question is asked of you by the public, it should be disregarded
    B. If you insist on formality between you and the public, the public will not be able to ask stupid questions that cannot be answered
    C. The public should be treated courteously, regardless of how stupid their questions may be
    D. You should explain to the public how stupid their questions are

12. With regard to public relations, the MOST important item which should be emphasized in an employee training program is that
    A. each inspector is a public relations agent
    B. an inspector should give the public all the information it asks for
    C. it is better to make mistakes and give erroneous information than to tell the public that you do not know the correct answer to their problem
    D. public relations is so specialized a field that only persons specially trained in it should consider it

13. Members of the public frequently ask about departmental procedures. Of the following, it is BEST to
    A. advise the public to put the question in writing so that he can get a proper formal reply
    B. refuse to answer because this is a confidential matter
    C. explain the procedure as briefly as possible
    D. attempt to avoid the issue by discussing other matters

14. The effectiveness of a public relations program in a public agency such as the authority is BEST indicated by the
    A. amount of mass media publicity favorable to the policies of the authority
    B. morale of those employees who directly serve the patrons of the authority
    C. public's understanding and support of the authority's program and policies
    D. number of complaint received by the authority from patrons using its facilities

15. In an attempt to improve public opinion about a certain idea, the BEST course of action for an agency to take would be to present the
    A. clearest statements of the idea even though the language is somewhat technical
    B. idea as the result of long-term studies
    C. idea in association with something familiar to most people
    D. idea as the viewpoint of the majority leaders

16. The fundamental factor in any agency's community relations program is
    A. an outline of the objectives
    B. relations with the media
    C. the everyday actions of the employees
    D. a well-planned supervisory program

17. The FUNDAMENTAL factor in the success of a community relations program is
    A. true commitment by the community
    B. true commitment by the administration
    C. a well-planned, systematic approach
    D. the actions of individuals in their contacts with the public

18. The statement below which is LEAST correct is:
    A. Because of selection standards, the supervisor frequently encounters problems resulting from subordinates' inability to express themselves in the language of the profession.
    B. Distortion of the meaning of a communication is usually brought about by a failure to use language that has a precise meaning to others.
    C. The term *filtering* is the distortion or dilution of content of a communication that occurs as information is passed from individual to individual.
    D. The complexity of the *communications net* will directly affect.

19. Consider the following three statements that may or may not be CORRECT:
    I. In order to prevent the stifling of communications flow, supervisors should insist that employees use the formal communications network.
    II. Two-way communications are faster and more accurate than one-way communications.
    III. There is a direct correlation between the effectiveness of communications and the total setting in which they occur.
    The choice below which MOST accurately describes the above statement is:
    A. All three are correct.
    B. All three are incorrect.
    C. More than one statement is correct.
    D. Only one of the statements is correct.

20. The statement below which is MOST inaccurate is:
    A. The supervisor's most important tool in learning whether or not he is communicating well is feedback.
    B. Follow-up is essential if useful feedback is to be obtained.
    C. Subordinates are entitled, as a matter of right, to explanations from management concerning the reasons for orders or directives.
    D. A skilled supervisor is often able to use the grapevine to good advantage.

21. *Since concurrence by those affected is not sought, this kind of communication can be issued with relative ease.*
    The kind of communication being referred to in this quotation is
    A. autocratic    B. democratic    C. directive    D. free-rein

22. The statement below which is LEAST correct is:
    A. Clarity is more important in oral communicating than in written since the readers of a written communication can read it over again.
    B. Excessive use of abbreviations in written communications should be avoided.
    C. Short sentences with simple words are preferred over complex sentences and difficult words in a written communication.
    D. The *newspaper* style of writing ordinarily simplifies expression and facilitates understanding.

23. Which one of the following is the MOST important factor for the department to consider in building a good public image?
    A. A good working relationship with the news media
    B. An efficient community relations program
    C. An efficient system for handling citizen complaints
    D. The proper maintenance of facilities and equipment
    E. The behavior of individuals in their contacts with the public.

24. It has been said that the ability to communicate clearly and concisely is the MOST important single skill of the supervisor.
    Consider the following statements:
    I.  The adage, *Actions speak louder than words*, has NO application in superior/subordinate communications since good communications are accomplished with words.
    II. The environment in which a communication takes place will *rarely* determine its effect.
    III. Words are symbolic representations which must be associated with past experience or else they are meaningless.
    The choice below which MOST accurately describes the above statements is:
    A. I, II, and III are correct.
    B. I and II are correct, but III is not.
    C. I and III are correct, but II is not.
    D. III is correct, but I and II are not.
    E. I, II, and III are incorrect.

25. According to expert opinion, the effectiveness of an organization is very dependent upon good upward, downward, and lateral communications. Lateral communications are most important to the activity of coordinating the efforts of organizational units. Before real communication can take place at any level, barriers to communication must be recognized, understood, and removed.
    Consider the following three statements:
    I.  The *principal* barrier to good communications is a failure to establish empathy between sender and receiver.
    II. The difference in status or rank between the sender and receiver of a communication may be a communications barrier.
    III. Communications are easier if they travel upward from subordinate to superior
    The choice below which MOST accurately describes the above statements is:
    A. I, II and III are incorrect.            B. I and II are incorrect.
    C. I, II, and III are correct.             D. I and II are correct.
    E. I and III are incorrect.

## KEY (CORRECT ANSWERS)

| | | | |
|---|---|---|---|
| 1. | B | 11. | C |
| 2. | D | 12. | A |
| 3. | A | 13. | C |
| 4. | A | 14. | C |
| 5. | D | 15. | C |
| | | | |
| 6. | D | 16. | C |
| 7. | A | 17. | D |
| 8. | D | 18. | A |
| 9. | A | 19. | D |
| 10. | A | 20. | C |

| | |
|---|---|
| 21. | A |
| 22. | A |
| 23. | E |
| 24. | D |
| 25. | E |

# EXAMINATION SECTION
## TEST 1

DIRECTIONS: Each question or incomplete statement is followed by several suggested answers or completions. Select the one that BEST answers the question or completes the statement. *PRINT THE LETTER OF THE CORRECT ANSWER IN THE SPACE AT THE RIGHT.*

1. Each of the following is one of the first considerations public relations practitioners should make when selecting the appropriate medium for message distribution EXCEPT  1.____

    A. target audience
    B. date at which audience needs to be reached
    C. possible combinations of media
    D. costs

2. Which phase of the diffusion cycle of persuasive information would occur LAST?  2.____

    A. Evaluation          B. Trial
    C. Awareness           D. Adoption

3. Which of the following is NOT considered to be one of the important psychological dimensions of public opinion?  3.____

    A. Intensity      B. Duration      C. Direction      D. Breadth

4. The _____ persuasion model is specifically designed to study the fact that an effective message is a message that causes a desired behavior from a person.  4.____

    A. symbolic interactionism
    B. structural functionalism
    C. sociocultural paradigm
    D. psychodynamic

5. The tryout of a public relations message on a small audience before general distribution is referred to as a  5.____

    A. release      B. pilot      C. hype      D. plant

6. Which of the following is NOT a title name typically held by government public relations practitioners?  6.____

    A. Public information officer
    B. Press secretary
    C. Director of public affairs
    D. Public relations representative

7. Which persuasive strategy involves creating a need or stimulating a desire?  7.____

    A. Cognitive              B. Social appeal
    C. Stimulus-response      D. Motivational

8. Which of the following is an advantage associated with the use of point-of-purchase displays as a medium for public relations communication?  8.____

A. Low unit cost
B. Creative flexibility
C. Involvement of dealer as partner in display
D. Short production time

9. The _____ model of public relations practice is MOST commonly used by businesses in highly competitive markets?

   A. press agentry/publicity  B. public information
   C. two-way asymmetric  D. two-way symmetric

10. Which of the following types of measurements would be used to determine the potency dimensions of a message?

    A. Loud-soft  B. Interesting-uninteresting
    C. Easy-difficult  D. Active-passive

11. A publicist whose assignment is to place clients with prominent public events is known as a(n)

    A. booker  B. planter
    C. gatekeeper  D. agenda-setter

12. Which of the following is considered a rule for executives or public relations representatives being publicly interviewed?

    A. Use expert talk for credibility
    B. Offer to help reporter in the future
    C. Avoid touchy questions
    D. Avoid off-the-record remarks

13. Which of the following is considered by public relations businesses to be a *nonchargeable* expense?

    A. Interviews, surveys, and placement of materials
    B. The supervision of mailing and distribution of releases
    C. Social activities with clients
    D. Travel time

14. Which of the following is NOT considered to be one of the learning principles associated with consumer behaviors?

    A. Appeals made over an extended period of time are most effective.
    B. Repetition is more effective when related to satisfaction and belongingness.
    C. Knowledge of results increases learning of a message.
    D. Learning a new pattern of behavior often reinforces the patterns already developed.

15. Each of the following is an objective of most public relations organizations (i.e., the Council for Advancement and Support of Education) related to schools and colleges EXCEPT

    A. developing gift and expenditure standards
    B. direct recruitment for athletics and other extracurricular programs
    C. improving the communication of university research to the public
    D. helping minority leaders at institutions to advance their careers

16. _____ is considered a propaganda technique.

    A. Social validation  B. Transfer
    C. Suggestion of action  D. Clarification

17. Of the steps in a problem-oriented public relations campaign listed below, which would occur LAST?

    A. Determine communications strategy
    B. Evaluation of problem's impact
    C. Development of organizational strategy
    D. Deciding upon tactics

18. An organization's image is conveyed to the public and evaluated in each of the following areas EXCEPT

    A. financial responsibility
    B. ability to form public policy
    C. ethics
    D. social responsibility

19. Which of the following statements does NOT reflect a public relations principle used to help organizations to maintain favorable public opinion?

    A. The economic and social stability of an organization is dependent upon the attitudes of the public within its operational environment.
    B. Technology should be avoided at all costs to avoid distancing the organization from the public.
    C. An organization's management of communications is essential to its ultimate ability to adjust to changes necessary for longevity.
    D. All individuals have the right to information about pending decisions relating to them or their welfare.

20. Which communication theory claims that a society's groups have competing needs and interests?

    A. Evolutionary perspective
    B. Structural functionalism
    C. Sociocultural paradigm
    D. Social conflict

21. _____ is a disadvantage associated with the use of pamphlets and booklets as a medium for public relations communication.

    A. Poor color reproduction
    B. The lack of opportunity for consumer referral
    C. Difficulty in measuring effectiveness
    D. Presentation of nonspecific messages

22. In terms of psychographic research, which of the following personality types would be considered inner-directed?

    A. Achievers  B. Emulators
    C. Need-driven  D. Belongers

23. According to the conditional probability theory of message receptiveness, which type of public is the MOST cost-effective for message distribution?
    A(n) _____ public characterized by _____.

    A. latent; constrained behaviors
    B. active; routine behaviors
    C. active; problem-facing behaviors
    D. aware; problem-facing behaviors

24. Which of the following is NOT typically one of the problems associated with an organization's internal publications?

    A. Too much space devoted to coverage of negative issues
    B. Little attempt to show how departments inter-relate
    C. Too office-oriented
    D. Not adequately funded

25. The type of survey in which every member of the targeted audience has a chance of being selected for questioning is the _____ sample.

    A. quota            B. purposive
    C. probability      D. social

---

# KEY (CORRECT ANSWERS)

| | | | |
|---|---|---|---|
| 1. | C | 11. | A |
| 2. | D | 12. | B |
| 3. | B | 13. | C |
| 4. | D | 14. | D |
| 5. | B | 15. | B |
| 6. | D | 16. | B |
| 7. | D | 17. | D |
| 8. | B | 18. | B |
| 9. | C | 19. | B |
| 10. | A | 20. | D |

21. C
22. C
23. D
24. A
25. C

# TEST 2

DIRECTIONS: Each question or incomplete statement is followed by several suggested answers or completions. Select the one that BEST answers the question or completes the statement. *PRINT THE LETTER OF THE CORRECT ANSWER IN THE SPACE AT THE RIGHT.*

1. Increasing _____ is NOT a factor leading to the growth of the governmental information effort.

    A. citizen demand
    B. complexity of society
    C. rural population
    D. public scrutiny

    1.____

2. When scheduling the preparation of public service announcements, APPROXIMATELY how much time should be set aside for the on-set shooting of the spot?

    A. 2-4 hours
    B. 4-8 hours
    C. 8-14 hours
    D. 2-3 days

    2.____

3. Which of the following types of studies is used to measure audience attitudes before and after a public relations campaign?

    A. Quota sampling
    B. Benchmark study
    C. Copy testing
    D. Retrieval study

    3.____

4. Which of the following is NOT a role of the public relations person during an interview?

    A. Preparer
    B. Questioner
    C. Facilitator
    D. Clarifier

    4.____

5. A review to determine public relations material and its relation to the target audience is

    A. probability sampling
    B. issues management
    C. a communication audit
    D. an institutional advertisement

    5.____

6. Each of the following is a guideline for publicity photographs EXCEPT

    A. always keep the number of subjects above three
    B. keep the background neutral
    C. position subjects close together
    D. high contrast

    6.____

7. The tendency of survey respondents to offer socially *correct* answers rather than ones disclosing their true opinions is known as

    A. courtesy bias
    B. transfer
    C. encoding
    D. flacking

    7.____

8. Which of the following is a problem specific to the practice of international public relations?

    A. The containment of crises
    B. Difficulty in monitoring potentially adverse situations
    C. An awkwardly long chain of command
    D. Difficulty in maintaining a favorable climate for operations

    8.____

9. Which persuasive strategy is MOST often used in an attempt to alleviate conditions for the poor and needy?

    A. Cognitive
    B. Social appeal
    C. Stimulus-response
    D. Motivational

10. The model of public relations practice MOST likely to involve withholding information from the public is the _____ model.

    A. press agentry/publicity
    B. public information
    C. two-way asymmetric
    D. two-way symmetric

11. In relation to social services, public relations techniques are considered essential to each of the following practices EXCEPT

    A. personnel
    B. client services
    C. fund-raising
    D. enlistment of volunteers

12. Of the steps in scheduling an annual report listed below, which would occur LAST?

    A. Producing copy
    B. Assigning work
    C. Clearing material recommendations
    D. Production

13. Public relations organizations working in the United States for other nations can expect to perform each of the following tasks EXCEPT

    A. advance political objectives
    B. assist in communications in the country's own language
    C. counsel the country about possible United States reactions to activities
    D. help modify laws and regulations inhibiting client's activities in the United States

14. Which method for determining client charges is MOST commonly used by public relations practitioners?

    A. Hourly fee
    B. Fee for services and out-of-pocket expenses
    C. Fixed fee
    D. Retainer

15. What is the term for the survey technique in which multiple samplings drawn from the same population are studied longitudinally and then compared or contrasted?

    A. Census
    B. Cohort study
    C. Bridge study
    D. Coincidental interview

16. The communication theory which claims that social change follows a set of natural laws is called

    A. evolutionary perspective
    B. structural functionalism
    C. sociocultural paradigm
    D. social conflict

17. Which of the following is NOT an advantage associated with electronically communicated information?

    A. Exists as part of people's everyday lives
    B. Often shows events happening, as well as reports them
    C. Immediacy of message
    D. Can selectively reach desired audiences

18. Which of the following is an element of off-premise community relations, as practiced by the administration of an organization?

    A. Talks to area organizations
    B. Anniversary celebrations
    C. Corporate disclosure
    D. Tables for fundraising

19. The pursuit of management objectives through suggestions, recommendation, and advice is the _____ function.

    A. line            B. transfer
    C. transfer        D. institutional

20. A typical public relations practitioner spends the LEAST amount of his/her professional time with

    A. lobbying
    B. media contacts/press conferences
    C. radio/television appearances
    D. meetings with outside groups

21. Which of the following is NOT a rule for executives or public relations representatives being publicly interviewed?

    A. Encourage hypothetical questions
    B. Avoid injecting yourself into the process during the actual interview
    C. Admit to not knowing the answer to some questions
    D. Answer questions that are public record

22. Which of the following is NOT generally considered a factor in determining the difficulty of an organization's internal communications?

    A. More sources such as television to divert workers' attention
    B. Increasing two-income families dilute one's interest in his/her job
    C. Increase in childbirth rate has produced competing responsibilities
    D. Increasing mobility of workers

23. The selection of a group to be polled that matches the characteristics of the entire audience is known as _____ sampling.

    A. probability     B. internal
    C. quota           D. purposive

24. The MOST important consideration in planning the composition of an annual report is

    A. scheduling      B. photography assignments
    C. distribution    D. printing procedures

25. Which of the following is NOT an objective of government information efforts?  25._____
    A. Represent the public and present its interests to representatives
    B. Advise government management on how best to communicate a decision or program
    C. Lobby for legislation supported by public opinion polls
    D. Educate administrators and bureaucrats about the role of mass media

## KEY (CORRECT ANSWERS)

| | | | |
|---|---|---|---|
| 1. | C | 11. | A |
| 2. | C | 12. | D |
| 3. | B | 13. | B |
| 4. | C | 14. | B |
| 5. | C | 15. | B |
| 6. | A | 16. | A |
| 7. | A | 17. | D |
| 8. | C | 18. | C |
| 9. | B | 19. | C |
| 10. | A | 20. | A |

21. A
22. C
23. C
24. A
25. C

# EXAMINATION SECTION
## TEST 1

DIRECTIONS: Each question or incomplete statement is followed by several suggested answers or completions. Select the one that BEST answers the question or completes the statement. *PRINT THE LETTER OF THE CORRECT ANSWER IN THE SPACE AT THE RIGHT.*

1. The model of public relations practice MOST commonly used by government agencies is the _____ model.

    A. press agentry/publicity
    B. public information
    C. two-way asymmetric
    D. two-way symmetric

2. Each of the following is one of the four primary areas of government-related public relations practice EXCEPT

    A. politics
    B. special interests inside government
    C. lobbying
    D. public affairs

3. Which of the following statements is considered to be one of the learning principles associated with consumer behaviors?

    A. It is easier to recall an appeal than to recognize it.
    B. Appeals made in exhaustive, momentary bursts of information are most effective.
    C. Unique messages are remembered more completely than others.
    D. Unpleasant appeals are usually not learned as well as pleasant ones.

4. Which phase of the diffusion cycle of persuasive information would occur FIRST?

    A. Information
    B. Adoption
    C. Reinforcement
    D. Awareness

5. Which of the following is a guideline associated with researching public relations campaigns associated with television or radio broadcasting?

    A. Design surveys to include primarily open-ended questions
    B. Attempt to cover the largest area possible
    C. Collect information by telephone or face-to-face interviews rather than by mail
    D. Gather information about subject's friends and family members, to conserve time

6. In which persuasive strategy is the cost-effectiveness of message repetition MOST problematic?

    A. Personality appeal
    B. Cognitive
    C. Stimulus-response
    D. Motivational

7. Which of the following is NOT one of the basic ideas behind the effort to influence public opinion?

    A. Reliability is difficult to assess
    B. Words, rather than events, are most likely to affect opinion
    C. Demands for action are a usual response
    D. Self-interest figures heavily into public involvement

8. _____ is categorized specifically as a *self-esteem* need that should be considered by the formers of a message.

   A. Knowledge
   B. Acceptance
   C. Intellectual curiosity
   D. Peace

9. Which of the following is NOT one of the personal characteristics considered necessary for a public relations practitioner?

   A. Intuition
   B. Specialized cultural background
   C. Training in the social sciences
   D. Objectivity

10. According to the basic principles of public relations, _____ is the sole criterion by which a public relations professional should be measured.

    A. versatility
    B. objectivity
    C. ethical performance
    D. demonstrated influence

11. Which method for determining client charges for public relations services is considered to be the RISKIEST?

    A. Hourly fee
    B. Fee for services and out-of-pocket expenses
    C. Fixed fee
    D. Retainer

12. According to the conditional probability theory of message receptiveness, the _____ public is among the secondary, rather than primary, group to target with a message.

    A. aware
    B. active
    C. latent
    D. latent/aware

13. The Public Relations Society of America's Code of Professional Standards defines political public relations as relating to each of the following EXCEPT the counseling of

    A. candidates or political organizations
    B. clients in connection with the client's relationship with government, with the purpose of influencing legislation
    C. media personnel who want to learn more about a candidate or political organization's record
    D. holders of public office

14. Which of the following is considered by public relations businesses to be a chargeable expense?

    A. Meetings with clients to prepare account material
    B. Maintaining contacts with media representatives
    C. Meetings with staff and other group conferences related to public relations business
    D. Preparation of materials for potential clients

15. Of the steps in a problem-oriented public relations campaign listed below, which would occur FIRST?  15.____

    A. Determine communications strategy
    B. Evaluation of problem's impact
    C. Development of organizational strategy
    D. Deciding upon tactics

16. Which function of a public relations practitioner involves analyzing problems and opportunities, as well as assigning responsibilities to appropriate personnel?  16.____

    A. Programming          B. Relationships
    C. Research and evaluation    D. Production

17. Which of the following is an advantage associated with the use of television as a medium for public relations communication?  17.____

    A. Good product identification
    B. Almost unlimited time allotment
    C. The creation of opportunities for consumer referral
    D. Low production costs

18. Which persuasive strategy is designed specifically for *outer-directed* people?  18.____

    A. Personality appeal       B. Social appeal
    C. Stimulus-response        D. Cognitive

19. The _____ model of public relations practice is characterized by an attempt to persuade the public to adopt the organization's point-of-view.  19.____

    A. press agentry/publicity    B. public information
    C. two-way asymmetric         D. two-way symmetric

20. Which of the following is one of the *laws* of public opinion?  20.____

    A. Opinion is basically determined by self-interest.
    B. Generally, public opinion is useful for the anticipation of emergencies.
    C. Opinion is usually sustainable through repetitive appeals.
    D. Generally, opinion is not sensitive to important events

21. In terms of psychographic research, which of the following personality types would be considered *outer-directed*?  21.____

    A. Sustainers        B. Achievers
    C. Experimentals     D. Survivors

22. Which of the following is a disadvantage associated with the use of radio as a medium for public relations communication?  22.____

    A. Time restrictions
    B. Neglect of local markets
    C. Relatively high production costs
    D. Difficulty in altering copy

23. Which of the following statements is NOT one of the basic principles of public relations practice?

   A. Public relations is primarily a service-oriented profession.
   B. Practitioners depend heavily on scientific public opinion research.
   C. Public relations is concerned not so much with reality as with the public's perception of reality.
   D. Practitioners depend largely on theories and practices of the social sciences.

24. The communication theory which claims that the stability of a society is dependent upon its organization is

   A. symbolic interactionism
   B. structural functionalism
   C. sociocultural paradigm
   D. social conflict

25. Which of the following types of measurements would be used to determine the ethical dimensions of a message?

   A. Powerful-weak
   B. Biased-unbiased
   C. Easy-difficult
   D. Active-passive

## KEY (CORRECT ANSWERS)

| | | | |
|---|---|---|---|
| 1. B | | 11. C | |
| 2. B | | 12. B | |
| 3. C | | 13. C | |
| 4. D | | 14. A | |
| 5. C | | 15. B | |
| 6. C | | 16. A | |
| 7. B | | 17. A | |
| 8. A | | 18. A | |
| 9. B | | 19. C | |
| 10. C | | 20. A | |

21. B
22. A
23. C
24. B
25. B

# TEST 2

DIRECTIONS: Each question or incomplete statement is followed by several suggested answers or completions. Select the one that BEST answers the question or completes the statement. *PRINT THE LETTER OF THE CORRECT ANSWER IN THE SPACE AT THE RIGHT.*

1. A typical public relations practitioner spends MOST of his/her professional time with     1.____

    A. lobbying
    B. media contacts/press conferences
    C. radio/television appearances
    D. speechmaking

2. Which of the following is an element of off-premise community relations, as practiced by the administration of an organization?     2.____

    A. Care for the handicapped and aged
    B. Open houses
    C. Offering free consultations
    D. Community bulletin boards

3. Each of the following is an explanation for the typically large budgets associated with the production of an annual report EXCEPT     3.____

    A. that it is the primary means by which most organizations communicate with the public
    B. high deadline pressures
    C. increasing regulation by the Securities and Exchange Commission
    D. that few other public relations methods practiced by the organization require much funding

4. What is the term for a speech written so that several speakers can deliver it to different audiences with only minor variations?     4.____

    A. Semantic     B. Basic     C. Pattern     D. Quota

5. Which of the following is NOT a reason for using the *inverted pyramid* style when writing public relations news releases?     5.____

    A. Good for hurried readers
    B. Will draw attention in opening lines
    C. Gives writer more room to present an idea or event
    D. Can usually be edited or cut without much loss of important information

6. Which of the following is NOT an objective of government information efforts?     6.____

    A. Explain agency techniques in a way that invites input from citizens
    B. Provide citizen feedback to government administrators
    C. Implement changes in the policies of government agencies, aligning with public opinion
    D. Communicate the work of government agencies

7. The model of public relations practice MOST commonly used by highly-regulated business, such as the telephone industry, is the _____ model.

    A. press agentry/publicity
    B. public information
    C. two-way asymmetric
    D. two-way symmetric

8. Which of the following is an advantage associated with the use of magazines as media for public relations communication?

    A. Domination of local markets
    B. Immediacy of message
    C. Nonselective targeting of audience
    D. Access to affluent consumers

9. Which persuasive strategy is designed specifically for people who have no negative preconceptions about the target behavior?

    A. Personality appeal
    B. Social appeal
    C. Motivational
    D. Cognitive

10. The pursuit of management objectives through supervision, delegation of authority, and work assignments is called the _____ function.

    A. line
    B. transfer
    C. staff
    D. institutional

11. Which of the following is NOT usually considered part of the necessary contents of internal publications?

    A. News stories
    B. Employee opinion forum
    C. Feature stories
    D. Items of record

12. In communications theory, the person or group that receives a message is known as the

    A. decoder
    B. gatekeeper
    C. encoder
    D. planter

13. When scheduling the preparation of public service announcements, APPROXIMATELY how much time should be set aside to allow for the choice of a cause or topic? _____ hours.

    A. 1-2    B. 2-4    C. 4-12    D. 8-16

14. Which of the following is NOT one of the *laws* of public opinion?

    A. People have more opinions with respect to goals than with respect to the means by which to achieve them.
    B. Public opinion is based more on information than desire.
    C. When opinion is not solidly structured, an accomplished fact tends to shift opinion in the accepted direction.
    D. Opinion is primarily reactive rather than proactive.

15. When a public relations practitioner selects opinion leaders to be interviewed, in order to insure the success of a campaign, this is known as _____ sampling.

    A. probability
    B. internal
    C. quota
    D. purposive

16. Which of the following is considered by public relations businesses to be a nonchargeable expense?

    A. Preparation of visual materials used in presentations
    B. Off-hours time spent with client personnel on client matters
    C. Professional development activities such as seminars
    D. Photographic assignments

17. Which of the following is NOT considered one of the ethical guidelines for people working in political public relations?
    Members shall not

    A. distribute advertising or publicity information which in unlabeled as to its source
    B. make gifts to influence decisions of voters or legislators
    C. engage in the inherently biased practice of partisan advocacy
    D. through information known to be misleading, intentionally injure the public reputation of the opposing candidate

18. A publicist who delivers new releases to media offices and urges their use is known as a(n)

    A. planter          B. encoder
    C. gatekeeper       D. booker

19. According to the conditional probability theory of message receptiveness, the most cost-effective for message distribution is a(n) _____ public characterized by _____ behaviors.

    A. latent/aware; constrained
    B. latent; routine
    C. active; problem-facing
    D. inactive; fatalistic

20. The communication theory which claims that the media's constructs of reality ultimately result in a society's individual and collective creations of reality is called

    A. symbolic interactionism
    B. social conflict
    C. evolutionary perspective
    D. psychodynamic model

21. Which of the following is an advantage associated with the use of direct mailing as a medium for public relations communication?

    A. Relaxed regulation of content
    B. Inexpensive
    C. Selectivity of target audience
    D. Consistency of mailing lists

22. Each of the following elements in a persuasive message is considered essential to provoking a response EXCEPT

    A. familiarity and trust     B. spirited challenge
    C. identification            D. suggestion of action

23. Which function of a public relations practitioner requires background knowledge of art, layout, and photography?  23.____

    A. Programming
    B. Information
    C. Research and evaluation
    D. Production

24. In researching public relations campaigns associated with television or radio broadcasting, what is generally considered to be the upper limit for the cross-section of the public necessary to provide an adequate information sample?  24.____

    A. 100        B. 500        C. 1,000        D. 5,000

25. Of the steps in scheduling an annual report listed below, which would occur FIRST?  25.____

    A. Producing copy
    B. Assigning work
    C. Clearing material recommendations
    D. Production

---

# KEY (CORRECT ANSWERS)

| | | | |
|---|---|---|---|
| 1. | B | 11. | B |
| 2. | A | 12. | A |
| 3. | D | 13. | C |
| 4. | C | 14. | D |
| 5. | C | 15. | B |
| 6. | C | 16. | C |
| 7. | D | 17. | C |
| 8. | D | 18. | A |
| 9. | D | 19. | A |
| 10. | A | 20. | A |

21. C
22. B
23. D
24. C
25. B

---

# EXAMINATION SECTION
# TEST 1

DIRECTIONS: In each of the following groups, one of the four sentences contains an error in grammar, usage, diction, or punctuation. Indicate the INCORRECT sentence. *PRINT THE LETTER OF THE CORRECT ANSWER IN THE SPACE AT THE RIGHT.*

1. 
   A. If I were you, he should not be allowed to regret having befriended the child.
   B. Deserted, surrounded and outnumbered, and with everything at stake, their refusal to surrender took great courage.
   C. Considering all his efforts in our behalf, our warmest thanks were clearly merited by him.
   D. He enjoyed, in his mountain retreat, not only skimming over the ice on his skates, but also feeling the danger of a mad rush down perilous slopes on his bobsled.

   1.____

2. 
   A. A young author is apt to run into a confusion of mixed metaphors which leaves the sense disjointed and the imagination distracted.
   B. We do not intend, in enforcing this rule, to guarantee your safety under all conditions; however, under ordinary circumstances, you will find you are adequately protected.
   C. When John entered the room, he shouted, "Run for your lives!" and then sat down quietly at the piano.
   D. My friend Eldridge has bought a plot of ground and intends to build a small house upon it within the year.

   2.____

3. 
   A. The students in the dormitories were forbidden, unless they had special passes, from staying out after 11:00 P.M.
   B. The Student Court rendered a decision satisfactory to both the defendant and the accuser.
   C. Margarine is being substituted for butter to a considerable extent.
   D. In this school there are at least fifteen minor accidents a year which are due to this traffic violation.

   3.____

4. 
   A. Everyone at camp must have his medical certificate on file before participating in competitive sports.
   B. A crate of oranges were sent from Florida for all the children in Cabin Six.
   C. John and Danny's room looks as if they were prepared for inspection.
   D. Three miles is too far for a young child to walk.

   4.____

5. 
   A. Sailing along New England's craggy coastline, you will relive a bygone era of far-roving whalers and graceful clipper ships.
   B. The march of history is reenacted in folk festivals, outdoor pageants, and fiestas local in theme, but national in import.
   C. Visiting the scenes of the past, our interest in American history is renewed and enlivened.
   D. What remained was a few unrecognizable fragments.

   5.____

6. A. The game over, the spectators rushed out on the field and tore down the goalposts.
   B. The situation was aggravated by disputes over the captaincy of the team.
   C. Yesterday they lay their uniforms aside with the usual end-of-the season regret.
   D. It is sometimes thought that politics is not for the high-minded.

6.____

7. A. Sandburg's autobiography, as well as his poems, are familiar to many readers.
   B. A series of authentic records of the American Indian tribes is being published.
   C. The Smokies are the home of the decendants of this brave tribe.
   D. Five dollars is really not too much to pay for a book of this type.

7.____

8. A. No one but her could have recognized him.
   B. She knew the stranger to be him whom she had given up as lost.
   C. He looked like he had been in some strange land where age advanced at a double pace.
   D. It is impossible to include that item; the agenda have already been mimeographed.

8.____

9. A. You have probably heard of the new innovation in the regular morning broadcast.
   B. During the broadcast you are expected to stand, to salute, and to sing the fourth stanza of "America."
   C. None of the rocks which form the solid crust of our planet is more than two billions years old.
   D. "I have finished my assignment," said the pupil. "May I go home now?"

9.____

10. A. The text makes the process of developing and sustaining a successful home zoo appear to be a pleasant profitable one.
    B. The warmth and humor, the clear characterization of the Walmsey family, which includes three children, two dogs, and two cats, is such fun to read that this reviewer found herself reading it all over again.
    C. You will be glad, I am sure, to give the book to whoever among your young friends has displayed an interest in animals.
    D. The consensus among critics of children's literature is that the book is well worth the purchase price.

10.____

11. A. Participation in active sports produces both release from tension as well as physical well-being.
    B. The problem of taxes is still with them.
    C. Every boy and every girl in the auditorium was thrilled when the color guard appeared.
    D. At length our club decided to send two representatives to the meeting, you and me.

11.____

12. A. B. Nelson & Co. has a sale of dacron shirts today.
    B. Venetian blinds-called that although they probably did not originate in Venice-are no longer used as extensively as they were at one time.
    C. He determined to be guided by the opinion of whoever spoke first.
    D. There is often disagreement as to whom is the better Shakespearean action, Evans or Gielgud.

12.____

13. A. Remains of an ancient civilization were found near Mexico City.
    B. It is interesting to compare the interior of one of the pyramids in Mexico to the interior of one of the pyramids in Egypt.
    C. In two days' journey you will be reminded of political upheavals comparable to the volcanic eruptions still visible and audible in parts of Mexico.
    D. There is little danger of the law's being broken, so drastic is the penalty.

    13.____

14. A. It did not take him long to develop an interest in the great American pastime - baseball.
    B. If you had made your way to the Whipsnade Zoo, you would have had an opportunity of seeing wild animals in more or less natural habitats.
    C. How I should have liked to have spent a few more days in Paris!
    D. Neither baseball pools nor any other form of gambling is allowed in or near the school.

    14.____

15. A. If the bill were introduced, it would provoke endless debate.
    B. Since George, with his two dogs, is to be with us, it might be better to rent a cabin.
    C. He, not I, is the one to decide.
    D. He is, however, one of those restless people who never seems content in his present environment.

    15.____

16. A. Instead of looking disdainfully at London grime, think of it as a mantle of tradition.
    B. Nobody but the pilot and the co-pilot was permitted to handle the mysterious package.
    C. Not only is industry anxious to hire all available engineers, but they are being offered commissions by the armed forces.
    D. For immediate service go direct to the store manager.

    16.____

17. A. The delegates alighted and started off in a taxi, their baggage having been taken care of.
    B. That kind of potatoes is grown in Idaho.
    C. Besides Alan Stevens, there were eight officers of the organization on the dais.
    D. As the delegates reached the convention hall late, they blamed their tardiness on the taxi driver.

    17.____

18. A. The new system is superior from every point of view to the inefficient system in use until now.
    B. The reason for the strike, you may recall, was because the union demanded a closed shop.
    C. Who's to decide whether it is to be installed?
    D. To suit Mr. Knolls, the new device will have to save time, money, and the dispositions of the employees.

    18.____

19. A. Everyone can have a wonderful time in New York if they will just not try to see the entire city in one week.
    B. Being a stranger in town myself, I know how you feel.
    C. New York City is a city of man-made wonders awe-inspiring as those found in nature.
    D. He felt deep despair (as who has not?) at the evidence of man's inhumanity to man.

    19.____

20. 
- A. In the recipe for custard, two cupfuls of milk will be enough.
- B. In the home economics classroom two tubs of clothes showed that it was not a day for cooking.
- C. It was 4:00 P.M. before the dishes were cleared away, washed, and put back into the closet.
- D. If only I had a fairy godmother like Cinderella!

20.____

21. 
- A. The zinnia has the more vivid color, but the violet is the sweeter-smelling.
- B. About three-fourths of the review I read was merely a summary of the story; the rest, criticism.
- C. I shall insist that he not be accepted as a member, since he is very bad-tempered.
- D. No sooner had he begun to speak when his auditors started to boo and hiss.

21.____

22. 
- A. The children's determination to find their dog almost resulted in tragedy.
- B. They spent the first night in a house that was unlocked and with no one at home.
- C. "What he asked me," said the boy, "was, 'Where can I find your father?'"
- D. It was the whimpering of a younger child and the comforting words of her brother that a member of the search-party heard about ten feet off the road.

22.____

23. 
- A. If I would have known how extraordinarily conscientious these visitors would be, I would have prepared a more elaborate trip.
- B. Enormous purchases of millinery are not warranted by business conditions in the large cities of this country.
- C. Joan studies English, physics, history, French, and algebra.
- D. I was asked which of the two books I liked better.

23.____

24. 
- A. When I reached the station, I discovered that I forgot my billfold.
- B. If Brutus had taken Cassius's advice, he would not have given Antony permission to speak.
- C. If John fails to help his mother, he will regret his selfishness.
- D. My father plans to visit the Philippines Islands in the fall, provided he can get accommodations on a steamer.

24.____

25. 
- A. There was something surreptitious and sacrilegious about his conduct: I didn't care for his personality at all.
- B. Since it is liable to rain, be sure to take your umbrella with you to the game.
- C. If he could ever remember consistently where he had laid important papers, he would assume that the millenium had arrived.
- D. There is no need to engage in self-flagellation each time you make an error; to err is human.

25.____

26. 
- A. In this cool room, neither the rose nor the gardenia will lose their freshness.
- B. Unless his persistent asceticism gets immediate psychiatric attention, the patient is very likely to find himself in a sanitarium.
- C. He has doubtless fully proven his innocence.
- D. Whether the Korean War has seriously affected the home front or not is a matter that needs further discussion.

26.____

27.  A. Confectioner's sugar is frequently used in baking.
     B. What happens when an immovable object meets an irrestible force?
     C. The principle reason for his objecting to any propitiatory gestures was that he was not a person who forgets an insult easily.
     D. He was operated upon for appendicitis.

27.____

28.  A. I read where the weather forecaster said a snow storm was coming.
     B. The thunder, not the flashes of lightning, frightens Janet.
     C. Harold doesn't study as I do.
     D. Thomas prefers that kind of grapes to any other on the market.

28.____

29.  A. From the position of the fingerprints, the detective inferred that the man who had fired the shot was left-handed.
     B. Do you know the name of the boy who sits next to you in our music class?
     C. He spared himself much embarrassment by returning back home.
     D. How serious a matter it is to try to resist, I have had ample opportunity to observe.

29.____

30.  A. My old friend and adviser is sick, I am sorry to say.
     B. Can you recall my telling you the story?
     C. He used a ten-foot pole in the pole vault, and very nearly broke the record.
     D. Obviously pleased, the assemblyman told the senator that he had been elected.

30.____

31.  A. His indifferent attitude and phlegmatic temperament contributed to the candidate's defeat in the plebiscite.
     B. We reached home, but the house was completely dark and we opened the door and saw Buster wagging his tail.
     C. With leaden feet Time creeps along.
     D. Jerry asked this question: "How should the ghost be represented on the stage?"

31.____

32.  A. The entire list of names of candidates was printed in the evening papers.
     B. If I should miss the train heaven forbid! I'll telephone you at once.
     C. During the current year, I have bought a new book every month.
     D. Since the bell did not ring yet, I plan to remain in the room for a while longer.

32.____

33.  A. I gave a folder to everybody present, not omitting myself.
     B. I was pleased delighted, I should say to hear your excellent report.
     C. The reason I have no pen is that I lent it to my assistant.
     D. Can you ever be sure that the person whom you know is a friend of yours today will be your friend tomorrow?

33.____

34.  A. Many colleges report that war veterans do work equal in quality to that of other students, or even better.
     B. I intend to be a lawyer because it is interesting work.
     C. Today the news is very disturbing, and we hear it through many avenues.
     D. How different he is from his younger brother!

34.____

35. A. In one aspect of the situation, Sam was better than any of the other men in his group; he could endure long hours, cold winds, and get drenched all day.
    B. No sooner had he entered the room than pandemonium broke loose.
    C. As a young man, I was incorrigible with respect to order; now that I am grown old, I feel very sensibly the want of it.
    D. If my father were as young as I, he would have a very different outlook on life.

36. A. Dickens' A TALE OF TWO CITIES is widely read in English classes.
    B. Give the book to whoever appeared first on line.
    C. Having borrowed over a thousand dollars, he was able to attend college for a year.
    D. 30 scientists listened in rapt attention to a succinct explanation of the function of chlorophyll.

37. A. These are the criteria for judging the merit of this composition.
    B. Aside from this error in punctuation, your composition is excellent.
    C. The sign on the road cautioned him to drive slow and to watch for children.
    D. The pupils asked permission to partake in the assembly program; however, they were refused.

38. A. He determined to enter and win the race.
    B. I find it difficult even to imagine a good excuse for his absence.
    C. Do you object to him joining us?
    D. If I were only there now, perhaps I might be able to help.

39. A. See that you attribute to no word a meaning different from the one it had a hundred years ago.
    B. No one could say for sure whether the scurrilous attack in the newspaper had brought on the cerebral hemorrhage.
    C. There were less pupils in the auditorium during the rehearsal for the school pageant than we had expected.
    D. When I saw that he wasn't working today, I realized fully the seriousness of his ailment.

40. A. When the President had finished his speech, everybody cheered; he lifted his hand in acknowledgment to them as he took his seat.
    B. I never heard of a woman's being offended by flattery.
    C. Some who have participated in military trials say it is not designed to promote justice for the defendant.
    D. Officers serving on court martial should peruse the documents with the utmost care.

41. A. Within his huge area is produced two-thirds the oats, more than half the corn, and half the wheat, wool and cotton.
    B. We can send you the refrigerator today, or we can keep it in the factory for a few days, if it is necessary to do so.
    C. Since his car is headed west, he'll not reach Maryland on that road.
    D. Never underestimate the value of a high school education.

42. A. All my friends were waiting when I arrived, and, despite my lateness, they greeted me courteously.
    B. He worked silently and swiftly, hoping to end his patient's discomfort quickly.
    C. Born in Salzburg, Mozart spent his childhood touring the cities of Europe.
    D. Please note the difference between "wither," "weather," "Whether," and "Whither."

42.____

43. A. Who did they say won?
    B. The man whom I thought was my friend deceived me.
    C. Send whoever will do the work.
    D. The question of who should be leader arose.

43.____

44. A. I will not go unless I receive a special invitation.
    B. The pilot shouted orders to his assistant as the plane burst into flames.
    C. She acts as though her feelings were hurt.
    D. Please come here and try and help me finish this piece of work.

44.____

45. A. Choose an author as you choose a friend.
    B. Home is home, be it ever so humble.
    C. You always look well in that sort of clothes.
    D. We had no sooner entered the room when the bell rung.

45.____

46. A. Never before, to the best of my recollection, have there been such promising students.
    B. It is only because your manners are so objectionable that you are not invited to the party.
    C. I fully expected that the children would be at their desks and to find them ready to begin work.
    D. A complete system of railroads covers the entire country.

46.____

47. A. The remainder of the time was spent in prayer.
    B. Immigration is when people come into a foreign country to live.
    C. He coughed continually last winter.
    D. The method is different from the one that was formerly used.

47.____

48. A. She is not nearly so clever as her older sister.
    B. In some ways our immediate ancestors differed but slightly from our primitive forebears.
    C. You had better pay close attention to the directions.
    D. This young cartoonist can draw as well or even better than a veteran artist.

48.____

49. A. Had the warden been more alert, the desperado would not have escaped so easily.
    B. "Come into my parlor," he said, "and make yourself at home."
    C. If we would have held out another week, the strike would have ended in our favor.
    D. The embattled troops rallied around that famous cry, "They shall not pass!"

49.____

50. A. Stroking his beard thoughtfully, an idea suddenly came to him.
    B. I read recently in an encyclopedia that Izaak Walton lived to the age of ninety.
    C. There are many reasons given for his success, his wit being most frequently mentioned.
    D. Having heard all the testimony in the case, the jury was charged by the judge.

50.____

# KEY (CORRECT ANSWERS)

| | | | | |
|---|---|---|---|---|
| 1. B | 11. A | 21. D | 31. B | 41. A |
| 2. A | 12. D | 22. B | 32. D | 42. D |
| 3. A | 13. B | 23. A | 33. D | 43. B |
| 4. B | 14. C | 24. A | 34. B | 44. D |
| 5. C | 15. D | 25. B | 35. A | 45. D |
| 6. C | 16. C | 26. A | 36. D | 46. C |
| 7. A | 17. D | 27. C | 37. D | 47. B |
| 8. C | 18. B | 28. A | 38. C | 48. D |
| 9. A | 19. A | 29. C | 39. C | 49. C |
| 10. B | 20. D | 30. D | 40. C | 50. A |

# TEST 2

DIRECTIONS: In each of the following groups, one of the four sentences contains an error in grammar, usage, diction, or punctuation. Indicate the INCORRECT sentence. *PRINT THE LETTER OF THE CORRECT ANSWER IN THE SPACE AT THE RIGHT.*

1. A. In recent years, the metals in many articles have been substituted by plastics.    1.____
   B. They are not in Boston now, but I think they're going to that city next week.
   C. The bag of peanuts was lost.
   D. His decision was firmly stated: there would be no more excursions.

2. A. There is, in these manifestations of distrust and suspicion, the very germ of dissension which may sprout into war.    2.____
   B. Whenever I read Somerset Maugham's OF HUMAN BONDAGE, I take a renewed interest in El Greco's art.
   C. The newest model of gun, as well as all previous models, have been made obsolete by atomic power.
   D. Neither machines nor manpower is lacking for the peaceful tasks that lie ahead.

3. A. There was, in the first place, no indication that a crime had been committed.    3.____
   B. She is taller than any other member of her class.
   C. She decided to leave the book lay on the table.
   D. Haven't you any film in stock at the present time?

4. A. The boys at camp liked swimming, boating, and to go on long hikes.    4.____
   B. The news of the victory was broadcast to all the soldiers in the field.
   C. He dived into the pool and swam to the opposite end.
   D. There were half a dozen people present who were attending the club's meeting for the first time.

5. A. Located on a mountainside with a babbling brook beside the door, it was a dream palace.    5.____
   B. Blessed are they who have not seen and yet have believed.
   C. The customs in that part of the country are much different than I expected.
   D. Politics, even in towns of small population, has always attracted ambitious young lawyers.

6. A. If John were here, he would help you solve the problem.    6.____
   B. Your statement that the report was not complete has aroused our suspicions.
   C. Every time I see you, you act like you're angry about something.
   D. Had he been your friend, he would have told you the plan.

7. A. I'm not feeling so good, may I lie down for a few minutes?    7.____
   B. Although the second attempt was somewhat better than the first, it was far from satisfactory.
   C. I wish I could play golf as well as he.
   D. We plan to meet my brother and her at the church.

89

8.  A. Baseball games, which are generally noisy, should not be played on the sand lot near the hospital.  8.____
    B. Boys, who work their way through school find it difficult to visit the library.
    C. They offered the prize to the girl who had the highest average for the term.
    D. This tall, anemic girl, who is considerably younger than she appears, has been undernourished since babyhood.

9.  A. She is somewhat disagreeable at home, but is always pleasant at school.  9.____
    B. During the entire night, we heard the mournful sound of the fog horn.
    C. Anyone can read the huge warning sign at the turn in the road, if they want to.
    D. The United States is a great country; its citizens should cherish its ideals of democracy.

10. A. If everyone does his duty, the plan will not fail.  10.____
    B. In the present situation, no one but I can help you.
    C. The sick man lay in bed all day, but rose in the evening to eat his dinner.
    D. I had begun to think I had lost my way, when suddenly I saw the paved highway.

11. A. Our vacation is over, I am sorry to say.  11.____
    B. It is so dark that I can't hardly see.
    C. Either you or I am right; we cannot both be right.
    D. After it had lain in the rain all night, it was not fit for use again.

12. A. The climate of New York is colder than California.  12.____
    B. I shall wait for you on the corner opposite the drug store.
    C. Here come my father and mother.
    D. Being a very modest person, John seldom talks about his invention.

13. A. My visit to Africa was fraught with untold perils.  13.____
    B. Visiting Montmartre is always an exciting adventure.
    C. Will there be a chance of you visiting Europe next year?
    D. Visiting me the other day, she explained why she had failed to leave them.

14. A. Do you remember when the late President Roosevelt said that "We have nothing to fear but fear itself?"  14.____
    B. Alas, how soon we grow forgetful of those rows of little white crosses all over the world!
    C. Mosquitoes have many larvae in stagnant pools; the best way to destroy them is to suffocate them by means of a film of oil spread over the water.
    D. "Please tell me," he politely interrupted, "whether you can spell 'Mississippi'."

15. A. If he were wealthy, he would build a hospital for the poor.  15.____
    B. I shall insist that he obey you.
    C. They believe it to be she who sent me the warning.
    D. What kind of cactus is this one?

16. A. When you go to the library tomorrow, please bring this book to the librarian in the reference room.  16.____
    B. His speech is so precise as to seem affected.
    C. I had sooner serve overseas than remain inactive at home.
    D. We read each other's letters.

17. A. John, a popular boy with many friends, was invited to spend a week at the camp.
    B. My failure was due to the poor method of study I employed at that time.
    C. When I graduated high school, I was only fifteen years old.
    D. We have a right to infer from your remarks that you think him guilty.

17.____

18. A. Ladies' hats are more expensive now than ever.
    B. They were frightened by his shrieking.
    C. They were grateful to whomever would help them.
    D. Large groups of persons visit the shrine every day.

18.____

19. A. On one side was a swamp, on the other a river.
    B. Take those books next door.
    C. Jack was running for our team when suddenly he drops the ball.
    D. The data which were used had been supplied by the agents.

19.____

20. A. Such consideration as you can give us will be appreciated.
    B. It looks to me like another World War will break out any minute.
    C. The boat sank at noon, but it was early evening before the first rescuers arrived on the spot.
    D. Microscopy is, with him, more than a fad.

20.____

21. A. Such participation, under wise leadership, has developed a sense of security and happiness in many citizens.
    B. He is here using the word "esquire" in the British sense of country gentlemen.
    C. We were sure, knowing him, that of the two alternatives, he would choose the one that was most difficult.
    D. It is true of Jim; it is true of Bill; it is true of Mary.

21.____

22. A. Neither opportunity nor ability has been absent from his career.
    B. The new era was brought about by us younger women.
    C. New York City is larger than any other city in the country.
    D. Anybody can sell this magazine in their neighborhood.

22.____

23. A. I am neither a villain, as has been alleged, or a coward.
    B. I wish I had been there when the incident occurred.
    C. He asked, "Shall you be twenty on your next birthday?"
    D. They went through all the formalities of a diplomatic function.

23.____

24. A. I can't understand Helen's making that mistake.
    B. He has lain there so long that he feels stiff all over.
    C. I don't know that we can go along.
    D. The reason why he had always avoided the honor of the Garter was because he knew that it cost a thousand pounds.

24.____

25. A. My brother detected the cause of the fire himself.
    B. Every sheet of white paper has been torn across the middle.
    C. The word "concurred" has been deleted and substituted by the word "dissented."
    D. This is a plain statement of fact endorsed by every diplomat now in Paris.

25.____

26.
   A. After all, consistency is the one important thing in business letter copy.
   B. I urged her to come down from off her high horse.
   C. A tattered flag hung all day from an attic window.
   D. There is nothing to puzzle you, because you don't have to send one penny or promise anything.

26.____

27.
   A. You are entirely right in your opinion about trespassing.
   B. He accepted the invitation because he enjoyed both fishing and to swim.
   C. All the sample books have thrilled countless readers.
   D. Getting down to brass tacks is difficult for my chief.

27.____

28.
   A. She objected to me reading so many novels and mystery stories.
   B. She is younger by many years than I.
   C. The ornateness of the paintings and the furnishings was not pleasing to my aesthetic sense.
   D. If you hadn't laid the book in the drawer, I should have had no difficulty in locating it.

28.____

29.
   A. Among the Bible stories that interest most people is the one about the battle between David and the giant, Goliath.
   B. They all arrived on time except you and I.
   C. She is so much taller than I, that I feel like a pigmy alongside her.
   D. I have always heard that the four years at college are the happiest years in a man's life.

29.____

30.
   A. We trusted to the sound of our footsteps on the gravel to keep us on the path.
   B. I have never been partial to those kind of newspapers.
   C. All suggestions pertaining to the improvement of conditions were considered from the standpoint of their practicability.
   D. My brother, with two of his friends, has joined the World Federalist movement.

30.____

31.
   A. While I was there I had many unpleasant experiences, some of which I shall never forget.
   B. Because he was independent of any political affiliation, his was a one-man campaign.
   C. The people cheered as soldier after soldier made their appearance.
   D. It is every citizen's duty first to register, and then to vote for the candidate best qualified.

31.____

32.
   A. The chairman, elected unanimously by the committee, has resigned.
   B. I shall give a copy of this pamphlet to whoever would like one.
   C. The boy should of completed his work the day before yesterday.
   D. Through all my troubles, I depended upon my roommate, than whom no stauncher friend exists.

32.____

33.
   A. Any of them is eligible to compete for the scholarship.
   B. Irregardless of your opinion, I feel inclined to be guided by my intuition.
   C. I should like everyone who I believe is capable to undertake this task.
   D. He was intent upon what he was doing and could not be distracted.

33.____

34. A. At the school at which she registered she will learn painting, dancing and to sing.
    B. Far out on the last jagged rock we could detect what appeared to be a wreck.
    C. She had, as those with strong natures always have, an unbounded confidence in her luck.
    D. Shaw made his first plunge into controversy: he rose to his feet, shaking with excitement, and heard himself speaking.

35. A. Neither the salary nor the work offers any great inducement to him.
    B. This property of my sister's is going to be sold soon.
    C. The temperature in Bermuda is almost never higher than Arizona or New Mexico.
    D. His satire on the corrupt society of the seventeenth century is subtly drawn.

36. A. Having eaten their lunch, the boat was quickly loaded and the picknickers departed.
    B. The materials were distributed among the four applicants.
    C. The man who was really responsible, the accountant, was arrested.
    D. "When did you arrive?" he asked.

37. A. The broiled fish looked good but tasted bad.
    B. The woman whom I believed to be his sister is his daughter.
    C. The last suggestion is more suitable than all that have been offered up to this point.
    D. The person who I always thought was my most dependable friend proved a great disappointment.

38. A. The scholarship was offered to whoever could show need of financial assistance.
    B. By applying himself diligently to the task, it was finally whipped into shape.
    C. This book has apparently lain undisturbed on the library shelf for many years.
    D. Weather prediction is based on data which are ascertained by means of sensitive instruments.

39. A. No answer having been received, it was assumed that Farley was no longer interested in the project.
    B. Neither the teachers nor the principal was discouraged by the results of the test.
    C. When engaged in reading, I do not like to be disturbed.
    D. Reading a few books thoughtfully is better than to skim many books superficially.

40. A. The pupil whom the faculty believed would win the essay contest failed to submit a paper.
    B. Bats are unable to see in the dark, yet avoid obstacles in a lightless cave.
    C. Luckily, none of the passengers in the wrecked plane was killed.
    D. None of Joan's class can draw more sensitively than she.

41. A. The rapid growth of television cannot but affect other media of mass entertainment.
    B. As a health resort, the high, dry air of the Rockies is always recommended for people suffering from lung trouble.
    C. Each of the children was given two teaspoonfuls of cod liver oil.
    D. "Ask Mr. Esposito," said Tom; "perhaps he can tell you."

42. A. The results of his investigations he embodied in three of the most brilliant essays he or any other Harvard graduate ever wrote.
    B. Whatever the consequences, my decision is irrevocable.
    C. If Barbara would have thought twice, she would not have spoken as she did.
    D. I think that you'll agree with me that CHARLOTTE'S WEB is one of the best children's books that have been published this year.

43. A. Mozart's chamber music, as well as his operas, are delightful to hear.
    B. The producer reported that he had recently read the revised third act and thought it excellent.
    C. Nobody but James and him was able to go to the Planetarium.
    D. The chimes rang true and sweet and gladdened the hearts of the listeners.

44. A. "Why," asked the magistrate, "did you pass the red light?"
    B. Respect for others, loyalty, integrity—these are the essential ingredients of good character.
    C. Be only satisfied with the best.
    D. If I were able to play a musical instrument, I should be very happy.

45. A. Doctors say that certain throat conditions are aggravated by smoking.
    B. When I hear someone speak of their thirteenth year as an unlucky year, I am irritated by the persistence of superstition.
    C. There are no words in English in which two c's follow the prefix re.
    D. Sir Toby Belch—he is the clown in TWELFTH NIGHT—is one of Shakespeare's most vivid characters.

46. A. The men's department is on the fifth floor, while the boys' is on the fourth.
    B. It was she whom the policeman had warned to remain on the sidewalk.
    C. Into every life come both joy and sorrow.
    D. The carton contained these items; a loaf of bread, a compass, a tattered diary, and a pair of muddy shoes.

47. A. The fact that Jones and Company reduced the amount of it's employees is no indication that there is a slump.
    B. I saw Mrs. Brown, her whom you pointed out at the meeting.
    C. John, that suit looks unusually good on you.
    D. We know the culprits to be them.

48. A. I don't see why he should feel so bad about his loss; its not as though he were impoverished.
    B. If he was honest, he would return the money.
    C. But for his uncle's intervention he would have been discharged.
    D. think they, on the average, are much heavier than we.

49. A. Conditions here are much better than Europe.
    B. The study of the changes that have taken place and the reasons for them is fascinating.
    C. I found the play exciting (and frightening), but the audience seemed unmoved by it.
    D. Neither of the boys was willing to go.

50. A. The lazy pupil, of course, will tend to write the minimum amount of words acceptable.
    B. The proposal that we should all go together was accepted enthusiastically.
    C. Had you heard the argument, you would be ready to excuse his anger.
    D. Dickens wrote DAVID COPPERFIELD; Thackeray, VANITY FAIR.

50.____

---

## KEY (CORRECT ANSWERS)

| | | | | |
|---|---|---|---|---|
| 1. A | 11. B | 21. C | 31. C | 41. B |
| 2. C | 12. A | 22. D | 32. C | 42. C |
| 3. C | 13. C | 23. A | 33. B | 43. A |
| 4. A | 14. A | 24. D | 34. A | 44. C |
| 5. C | 15. C | 25. C | 35. C | 45. B |
| 6. C | 16. A | 26. B | 36. A | 46. D |
| 7. A | 17. C | 27. B | 37. C | 47. A |
| 8. B | 18. C | 28. A | 38. B | 48. B |
| 9. C | 19. C | 29. B | 39. D | 49. A |
| 10. B | 20. B | 30. B | 40. A | 50. A |

# EXAMINATION SECTION
# TEST 1

DIRECTIONS: In each of the following groups of sentences, there are three sentences which are correct and one which is incorrect because it contains an error in grammar, usage, diction, or punctuation. Indicate the INCORRECT sentence. PRINT THE LETTER OF THE CORRECT ANSWER IN THE SPACE AT THE RIGHT.

1. 
   A. Take one of these books which are to be discarded because it has no value any more.
   B. Although the period has lasted for more than thirty minutes, the students are not tired and can do much more work.
   C. Williams has a most unique idea for the school play, and he plans to discuss it with his teacher.
   D. After cleaning the house, my mother lay in the hammock for an hour; then she went shopping.

   1.____

2. 
   A. Sunrise High School, with an enrollment of 1,200 boys and 1,100 girls, is the largest in the state.
   B. I was pleased with his visiting me in the hospital as I was lonely and depressed at the time.
   C. To type with your feet spread out in all directions is considered to be an example of poor typewriting technique.
   D. First-class furs like first-class diamonds are very expensive; both the initial cost and the year-to-year upkeep require a great deal of money.

   2.____

3. 
   A. Not having received a reply to my letter of June 8, I am writing again to ask if anything is wrong.
   B. She asked, "Whom does Mr. Jones feel should have won the typewriting medal?"
   C. Strawberries and cream is a perfect summer dessert, and I have asked my mother to serve the dish frequently.
   D. Either Mary or the boys have broken the window, and I mean to find out immediately before they do further damage.

   3.____

4. 
   A. Of the ladies present at the meeting, three were chosen to be delegates to the annual convention to be held the following May.
   B. The reason I succeeded is that I prepared thoroughly for the test.
   C. I heard her say that the window was broken by the ball and damaged the vase in the living room.
   D. They have been chosen for two reasons—namely, because they are intelligent and because they are conscientious.

   4.____

5. 
   A. Latin, French, and English, in that order, were my favorite subjects in high school.
   B. Since a stay of execution has not been received from the governor, the murderer must be hanged at midnight.
   C. Knowing that you want an immediate answer, I suggest that you send your request to Mr. Smith or to whoever is in charge of such matters.
   D. We ordered pencils and typewriter ribbons whichever were available from the stationer on the corner.

   5.____

6.  A. Business was not good; and becoming very irritated, the partners decided to close the store for the day.
    B. I am pleased with your work — work that shows through preparation and in your typewriting ability.
    C. The house was low and long and appeared to be newly built.
    D. This office is often used by salesmen who have nothing better to do, and especially by unsuccessful salesmen.

7.  A. Reading this well-written book was a never-to-be forgotten experience; I was both repelled and drawn toward the hero.
    B. I can hardly realize that in two weeks I shall be in Europe. The reason is that I have never traveled before.
    C. I want four only, but I will take five or six if you insist.
    D. Mrs. Jones plans to speak with Sally about her poor grades. The girl failed two subjects last month.

8.  A. Strictly speaking, he cannot be considered a good base ball player — or, for that matter, a good tennis player.
    B. To learn to type well, you should practice daily; to acquire high speed in shorthand, you should practice constantly.
    C. The teachers' committee consisted of Dr. Smith, the principal, Mr. Jones, the program committee chairman, Mrs. Greene, the senior grade adviser, and the administrative assistant.
    D. His secretary and Girl Friday was the most efficient worker he had ever hired, and he was delighted with her.

9.  A. There were but two of us left after examinations had been graded.
    B. Neither the two bushes nor the elm tree was damaged by the hurricane.
    C. "Did you go to the office?", Mary asked. "No," Sally replied, "and I don't intend to."
    D. The engine as well as the fenders and the wheels was severely damaged, and neither you nor I am prepared to say how much the repair bill will be.

10. A. I observed that the house was one of those rambling old mansions that one often sees in Southern towns.
    B. By concentrating on spelling while I am learning how to type, I am putting my time to better use.
    C. Please repeat the sentence again because none of the children in the rear heard you.
    D. The police have arrested three men: John Winters, 27, Brooklyn; Timothy Flynn, 26, Brooklyn; and Sheldon Young, 26, Queens.

11. A. "I have laid the book down," she said. "I shall now go to sleep."
    B. The policeman, not the gangsters, merits our approval despite the fact that crime is made to be so attractive on television.
    C. "Did you finish your composition yet?" Sally asked. "No," Jane replied.
    D. Where can I find out who wrote, "What you don't know would make a great book"?

12. A. I read in a book that boys and girls today are taller and heavier than their parents were at the same age. How interesting!
    B. John said that from where he was sitting in the ball park, he could hardly see the batter and the pitcher.
    C. He expects to be graduated from Morningside High School in January instead of June as he has been taking extra summer courses.
    D. Speaking of employment, have many new jobs been created on Long Island as a result of all the industries which have settled there during the past five years?

12.____

13. A. I have risen at five o'clock in the morning for the past twenty years, and I am still in excellent physical condition.
    B. I have laid the letter on my employer's desk several times, but he still has not signed it.
    C. We felt that if he would have tried harder, he might have passed the examination.
    D. I am angry with John principally because I am angry at the comments he made at the rally last night.

13.____

14. A. I met a friend of father's the other day in Boland and Ryan's suburban store.
    B. Less men were hurt this year than last because of the intensive safety precautions which have been introduced.
    C. During several months — that is, June, July, and August — school is closed.
    D. We need all types of skills in our office — for example stenographers, typists, IBM operators, duplicator operators, and typist-clerks.

14.____

15. A. The paper says that civil liberties is the principal topic of conversation in Washington today.
    B. I do not know why — but perhaps I shouldn't try to find out at this time.
    C. I would have preferred to do nothing until he came, so I decided to lie down.
    D. As I was entering the office, I heard a bell clang right behind me, which gave me a bad fright.

15.____

16. A. As I went deeper and deeper into the forest, the light became dimmer and dimmer.
    B. Did he actually say, "I can't do a thing for you"? I can imagine him being so ungrateful.
    C. After he had seen the play OKLAHOMA (which he had been told in advance was excellent), he decided to go to the theater much more often.
    D. Bill Carlton did not go to college, which shocked his family and astonished his friends because Bill was a really good student.

16.____

17. A. If Tom had worked all summer in a camp or in a restaurant, he might have saved enough money to buy a car.
    B. I am not sure which typewriter is liked better, the Royal or the IBM Selectric; and I plan, therefore, to look into the matter further.
    C. We stopped at John's house to see if his trophy was different from Mark's trophy.
    D. Tom said that he was going over to Sally's house after the school dance and that we should not expect him home until midnight.

17.____

18. A. Tom never has and never will obtain the grades required for admission to Harvard.  18.____
    B. The rain fell harder and harder as I walked away from home.
    C. "There is nothing to worry about dear," her mother answered quietly. "What a fuss you do get into! Heavens! Now take the nice medicine."
    D. The union leader, whom it was believed all the men admired, was, in fact, very much hated by most of them.

19. A. You had better not stay too long or you will get into trouble—unless, of course, you just don't care.  19.____
    B. His latest book The Psychology of Mental Life was published in 1991. Have you read his other books?
    C. The clerk whom I thought to be the best was, in actuality, the worst.
    D. He said that he sold: typewriters, adding machines, mail equipment, and time clocks.

20. A. There was danger of the enemy attacking from the rear and destroying our army before we could bring up the necessary reserves.  20.____
    B. There were approximately ten applicants in the office waiting to be interviewed for the job.
    C. He acts, it seems to me, as though he were guilty.
    D. We have studied John Smith's, William Wilson's, and Tom Blake's claims; and we feel quite sure that they will soon be settled.

21. A. He is a person who pleases you the moment you meet him, so that you want to be with him and to know him better.  21.____
    B. He had no love for, nor confidence in, his employer.
    C. First type the letter and then you should put it in the envelope.
    D. His salary was lower than a typist's, but he did not care because there were excellent opportunities for advancement.

22. A. I typed this letter – you may not believe this, but it is true – in four minutes.  22.____
    B. "It is clear (the message read) that the Muscle Shoals development is but a small part of the potential public usefulness of the entire Tennessee River."–D.E. Lilienthal
    C. Shaw made his first plunge into controversy: he rose to his feet, shaking with nerves and heard himself speaking.
    D. After the reading of the will, he opened up the strong box and divided up the money among the relatives present.

23. A. Dissatisfaction with the theoretical bases and practical workings of the general property tax has given rise to two movements of tax reform.  23.____
    B. Let the book lie on the table.
    C. Since the department is reducing its number of employees is not proof that they are not needed.
    D. Who do you think will be selected for the position?

24. A. Application of the principles discovered during those experiments have been of great value to mankind.  24.____
    B. Every one of the editorial assistants proved his worth without exception.
    C. State regulation of morals aids in the protection of the family.
    D. Working when one is tired does not yield the best results.

25. A. We learned that there was more than ten people present at the conference.
    B. Every one of the employees is able to lift the carton.
    C. Neither the registrar nor the secretary is in the office today.
    D. The administrative assistant stated that any office assistant who stayed overtime tonight would get a half-day off next month.

25._____

---

## KEY (CORRECT ANSWERS)

| | | | |
|---|---|---|---|
| 1. | C | 11. | C |
| 2. | D | 12. | B |
| 3. | B | 13. | C |
| 4. | C | 14. | B |
| 5. | D | 15. | D |
| 6. | B | 16. | B |
| 7. | A | 17. | D |
| 8. | C | 18. | A |
| 9. | C | 19. | D |
| 10. | C | 20. | A |

| | |
|---|---|
| 21. | C |
| 22. | D |
| 23. | C |
| 24. | A |
| 25. | A |

---

# TEST 2

DIRECTIONS: In each of the following groups of sentences, there are three sentences which are correct and one which is incorrect because it contains an error in grammar, usage, diction, or punctuation. Indicate the INCORRECT sentence. *PRINT THE LETTER OF THE CORRECT ANSWER IN THE SPACE AT THE RIGHT.*

1. A. I read political science books as a kind of a duty, not for pleasure.
   B. You needn't go to all that expense for me.
   C. It will be extremely interesting to note the varied reactions of the other participants.
   D. Please do not be angry with me, because it really was not my fault.

2. A. We go there by boat and return by train.
   B. He wrote home for his bathing trunks, tennis racket, and set of golf clubs.
   C. Take me to his home, and I will tell him myself.
   D. The autobiography of George Bernard Shaw by Ernest Jones was assigned for reading by my English teacher.

3. A. Everyone was given his fair share.
   B. If the river will rise much higher, we may have a flood.
   C. There were, in the early years of this century, many more horses than automobiles.
   D. Either your enunciation is faulty or I am hard of hearing.

4. A. The boy assured his teacher that he would pass the tests with ease.
   B. Every person in these two buildings has to meet their responsibilities.
   C. Thunderstorms will invariably follow a lengthy hot spell.
   D. I believe the boy to be him.

5. A. I lay it on the bench before I left.
   B. She wrung the clothes before she bought a washing machine.
   C. We have drunk all the water.
   D. The wind has blown like this all night.

6. A. I like Shakespeare's HAMLET better than any of his plays.
   B. The roads are in poor condition because of the torrential rains.
   C. They robbed the child.
   D. They have stolen my cash.

7. A. If the winner of the contest were here, I would give him his medal.
   B. I hope my son graduates junior high school next June.
   C. Now is the time to make sure that we have beaten that team.
   D. We believe that those books are up to date.

8. A. Be careful that you do not slip on that oily surface.
   B. I hope to be able to take notes during his worthwhile lecture.
   C. I think that phenomena is worth photographing.
   D. It occurred in the 1960s, not during the 1950s.

9.  A. New York is larger than any city in Europe.
    B. Just as we reached the boat landing, the weather changed.
    C. Coming around the curve, the large house was seen.
    D. Generally speaking, my daughter is a good student.

10. A. Place the children's toys above the others.
    B. It was more unique that I thought it would be.
    C. It was my opinion, albeit an erroneous one, that he was the best swimmer on the team.
    D. The typewriter's ribbon was frayed.

11. A. The chances are that Ted's relatives believe in his honesty.
    B. I am glad that you think this was so.
    C. Give it to the club to which my grandmother belongs.
    D. I am in New York for ten years.

12. A. I have heard that he is never returning.
    B. In the last century it was especially fashionable to dress in that manner.
    C. This data, in my opinion, is incorrect.
    D. It is a highly selective procedure which must be followed.

13. A. She sat besides me on the couch.
    B. Billy is the best Spanish scholar of the three boys.
    C. It is gratifying to know that the city school system's strengths are being publicized.
    D. I do not have very much faith in his changing his mind.

14. A. I think that he should be feeling somewhat better.
    B. Do as she does if you want to do it correctly.
    C. I am surely glad that he was able to pass the test.
    D. Hide it some place.

15. A. He seemed to be possessed by an evil spirit.
    B. I think that his point of view is different from mine, but I still believe that I am correct.
    C. I agree to the new plan, but I disagree with him in regard to how it is to be accomplished.
    D. He has the natural desire to be independent from his parents.

16. A. Whenever she went to school she learned a lot.
    B. We had hoped to be on time, but we were late.
    C. My greatest fear, however, was overcome at the last moment.
    D. The two painters' works were displayed at the gallery.

17. A. The check from the Treasury Department will arrive on Monday, January 23.
    B. James was not sure that it was Jane and me at the party.
    C. I do not know if the search for William and her has been made.
    D. There were many accidents on the highway, but the toll was less than had been anticipated.

18.  A. A baby girl was just what we wanted.
    B. His vote was the larger of the two candidates.
    C. That boy had neither money or influence, and I do not know what chances of success he had.
    D. I may lie down on that bed if I get tired.

19.  A. He doesn't live too far from his friend's home.
    B. The northeast was covered with snow.
    C. Let's cut it into six portions so that we can each have a piece.
    D. The boy did six days' work.

20.  A. It was in first-class condition, and I decided to keep it.
    B. It was a highly polished piece of jewelry.
    C. The twins, not their little brother, has the measles.
    D. That is the most important document in the history of our country.

21.  A. Medical training in Greece has been modernized, and the younger doctors have either studied in the United States or Europe.
    B. He will not bring the car here without my telling him.
    C. He is as tall as, if not taller than, the teacher,
    D. If one is asked to count from one to five inclusive, he should count as follows: one, two, three, four, five.

22.  A. The leader of the movement is Mr. Harold L. Parne, Esq.
    B. He expects to be graduated from college next month.
    C. If one lives in Florida one day and in Iceland the next, he is certain to feel the change in temperature.
    D. He is the one of the boys who is always on time.

23.  A. Since only one in the jury responded to the foreman's question, he looked at them inquiringly.
    B. According to an old adage, every dog has its day.
    C. It was I whom he wanted to sing.
    D. Now that the stress of examinations and interviews are over, we can all relax for a while.

24.  A. The arrival of the letter was prior to that of the package.
    B. If you convey this suggestion back to your committee, we shall obtain a solution to our problem.
    C. They all looked different after their return from Vietnam.
    D. Illiteracy is the condition of the man who cannot read or write.

25.  A. Do you think we have paid too much? too little?
    B. Neither John nor I am to receive the reward.
    C. The farmer lost nearly one hundred cattle in the fire.
    D. We are making fewer mistakes with the new calculating machine.

# KEY (CORRECT ANSWERS)

1. A
2. D
3. B
4. B
5. A

6. A
7. B
8. C
9. C
10. B

11. D
12. C
13. A
14. D
15. D

16. A
17. B
18. C
19. B
20. C

21. A
22. A
23. D
24. B
25. A

# TEST 3

DIRECTIONS: In each of the following groups of sentences, one sentence is incorrect because it includes an error in grammar, usage, sentence structure, capitalization, diction, or punctuation. Indicate the INCORRECT sentence. *PRINT THE LETTER OF THE CORRECT ANSWER IN THE SPACE AT THE RIGHT.*

1. A. Her poor posture made taking dictation a fatiguing chore.
   B. The secretary promptly notified the principal of the fire for which she was highly praised.
   C. She makes too frequent use of correction fluid when she types stencils.
   D. Old records are sometimes kept in a basement storeroom.

1.___

2. A. She learned the uses of punctuation marks from one of the dictionary's appendixes.
   B. The administrative assistant acted as principal in the latter's absence.
   C. You see, you did mail the letter to yourself!
   D. We are impressed by her exemplary performance and industry; they are a stimulant to us to do better work.

2.___

3. A. The rotation of duties and responsibilities among the secretaries are highly desirable.
   B. The school secretary must remember to maintain contact with teachers assigned to the Board of Education.
   C. She could not operate the electric typewriter because she had not plugged it in.
   D. Eleanor utilized a postal scale to determine the cost of mailing the parcel.

3.___

4. A. Please list the names of alumnae from the year 1963 on.
   B. Her filing went like clockwork because of the prior alphabetizing of the folders.
   C. She let the phone ring for awhile, but when she finally answered, the line was dead.
   D. The secretary's merits were duly noted in the principal's report.

4.___

5. A. At closing time, one should not be short tempered with long-winded visitors.
   B. The eraser was lost after it had lain alongside the typewriter.
   C. Her spelling was as acceptable as theirs, if not more acceptable.
   D. We ordered many copies of Webster's new International dictionary from federal funds.

5.___

6. A. For the sake of expediency, we divided the work between the four of us.
   B. She quickly learnt to use a comptometer.
   C. Miss Smith would rather take dictation than operate the switchboard.
   D. The dimensions of the envelope determine the quantity of matter that may be enclosed.

6.___

7. A. Joan's suggestion for recording absences, though untried, seems practicable.
   B. The expression, "Thanking you in advance," is unacceptable in up-to-date correspondence.
   C. She informed latecomers not to feel badly because the snowstorm would be accepted as a valid excuse.
   D. The school secretary was pleased that the courses she had taken were relevant to her work.

7.___

8.  A. He was extremely kind to me yesterday.
    B. I talked to him in regard to the subscription.
    C. They were so good to me.
    D. The teacher spoke clear and emphatic.

9.  A. Our vacation is over, I am sorry to say.
    B. It is so dark that I can't hardly see.
    C. Either you or I am right; we cannot both be right.
    D. After it had lain in the rain all night, it was not fit for use again.

10. A. When either or both habits become fixed, the student improves.
    B. Neither his words nor his action was justifiable.
    C. A calm almost always comes before a storm.
    D. The gallery with all its pictures were destroyed.

11. A. Next summer I shall either travel by plane or by boat down to Bermuda.
    B. The reason Tom won the award is that he studied hard.
    C. Undoubtedly the best scene in the play occurs when the son confronts his mother.
    D. History is the record of events that have happened.

12. A. John was invited to spend a week at the camp.
    B. My failure was due to the poor method of study I employed at that time.
    C. When I left home, I was only fifteen years old.
    D. We imply from your remarks that you think him guilty.

13. A. The advantages of such an arrangement enables the teachers to plan her work more efficiently.
    B. Typing skill is the result merely of the acquisition of a number of habits.
    C. We are more likely to catch cold in overheated rooms than in chilly ones.
    D. Both political parties promise to balance the budget if and when they are elected to office.

14. A. They have neither the patience nor the skill necessary to solve these problems.
    B. This is the only decision that can be reached: either you or I are right.
    C. You should lend your book to the student who you think will enjoy reading it.
    D. The Red Cross is doing its utmost to provide medical supplies for the flood areas.

15. A. The driver sustained internal injuries.
    B. It is the only textbook of its kind that has, is, or may be published.
    C. Thinking speaking and writing are closely related learnings.
    D. Most of us recognize good English when we hear it or read it.

16. A. This sort of emergency always has its exciting moments.
    B. A tragic play is when the action ends unhappily.
    C. The committee adjourned sine die and went to their homes for a much needed rest.
    D. It is essential that you be on the alert at all times.

17. A. The reason he was late getting to work was because he overslept.    17.____
    B. As we read the daily newspaper headlines, a feeling of despair overwhelms us.
    C. His gentle speech is no proof that he is kind.
    D. Shall we lay the book on the table?

18. A. We want to travel extensively and have new experiences.    18.____
    B. Charles is my brother, James being my cousin.
    C. His teacher is one person in whom he can confide.
    D. The skater suddenly lost control and crashed into the rail.

19. A. Because he was sympathetic and tolerant, most people respected him.    19.____
    B. What are the principal points to be emphasized in the conduct of drill practice?
    C. The lecturer called attention to the beginning of the movement and how it ended.
    D. The average citizen has far more civic power than he realizes.

20. A. The committee has done their best to raise the money necessary to build the new club house.    20.____
    B. He was neither willing nor able to pay the exorbitant fee.
    C. We all want to be happy, and we want our fellow men to be happy.
    D. If ours were a totalitarian society, we would probably limit the number of pupils admitted to colleges.

21. A. The filling-out of the application blank took up one third of his time.    21.____
    B. The talent for brevity is given to few politicians!
    C. Dashing to the front window, the parade came into view.
    D. Each day this newspaper prints a summary of up-to-the-minute news on the front page.

22. A. Because of his ability as a leader, he was undoubtedly the man for the job.    22.____
    B. Not only were they disappointed but also angry.
    C. If one is to learn French well one must speak it regularly.
    D. The most famous collection of prayers known to history is the Book of Psalms.

23. A. We planned to stay a week in at Rocky Landing.    23.____
    B. The bus driver agreed to take as many as wanted to go.
    C. Any man may vote, be he rich or poor.
    D. The teacher assigned three of us, John, Sam, and I, to help with the arrangements for the party.

24. A. Today, more then ever, we need the steadying influence of stable homes and families.    24.____
    B. Was ever a man so tormented!
    C. This report — may it never be forgotten — is our last, our very last.
    D. The letter states, "I am agin(sic) every idea you have."

25. A. Although he must have known the answer, he refused to volunteer the information.    25.____
    B. The pirate captain divided up the booty among his crew according to their rank.
    C. As the gale gathered force, the captain mounted the bridge.
    D. As he threw the line over the side of the boat, he suddenly remembered that the rope was fouled.

## KEY (CORRECT ANSWERS)

| | | | |
|---|---|---|---|
| 1. | B | 11. | A |
| 2. | D | 12. | D |
| 3. | A | 13. | A |
| 4. | C | 14. | B |
| 5. | D | 15. | B |
| 6. | A | 16. | B |
| 7. | C | 17. | A |
| 8. | D | 18. | B |
| 9. | B | 19. | C |
| 10. | D | 20. | A |

21. C
22. B
23. D
24. A
25. B

# ENGLISH EXPRESSION
# EXAMINATION SECTION
## TEST 1

DIRECTIONS: Each question or incomplete statement is followed by several suggested answers or completions. Select the one that BEST answers the question or completes the statement. *PRINT THE LETTER OF THE CORRECT ANSWER IN THE SPACE AT THE RIGHT.*

Questions 1-9.

DIRECTIONS: The following sentences contain problems in grammar, usage diction (choice of words), and idiom. Some sentences are correct. No sentence contains more than one error. You will find that the error, if there is one, is underlined and lettered. Assume that all other elements of the sentence are correct and cannot be changed. In choosing answers, follow the requirements of standard written English. If there is an error, select the *one underlined* part that must be changed in order to make the sentence correct. If there is no error, mark E.

1. <u>In planning</u> your future, <u>one must be</u> as honest with yourself as possible, make careful     1.____
       A                        B
   decisions about the best course <u>to follow to achieve</u> a particular purpose, and, above all,
                                       C
   have the courage <u>to stand by those</u> decisions.  <u>No error</u>
                     D                   E

2. <u>Even though</u> history does not actually repeat itself, knowledge <u>of</u> history <u>can give</u>     2.____
       A                                                B      C
   current problems a familiar, <u>less</u> formidable look.  <u>No error</u>
                     D                   E

3. The Curies <u>had almost exhausted</u> their resources, and <u>for a time it seemed</u>     3.____
              A                                        B
   <u>unlikely that they ever</u> would find the <u>solvent to their financial problems</u>.  <u>No error</u>
            C                                  D                   E

4. <u>If the rumors are</u> correct, Deane <u>will not be convicted</u>, for each of the officers     4.____
        A                                  B
   on the court realizes that Colson and Holdman may be <u>the real culprit and</u> that
                                                                  C
   <u>their</u> testimony is not completely trustworthy.  <u>No error</u>
     D                                               E

5. The citizens of Washington, <u>like Los Angeles</u>, prefer to commute by automobile,
             A
   even though motor vehicles contribute <u>nearly as many</u> contaminants to the air
                 B
   <u>as do all other</u> sources <u>combined</u>. <u>No error</u>
     C      D    E

6. <u>By the time Robert Vasco completes</u> his testimony, every major executive of our
         A
   company but Ray Ashurst <u>and I</u> <u>will have been</u> <u>accused of</u> complicity in the stock
           B   C    D
   swindle. <u>No error</u>
       E

7. <u>Within six months</u> the store was operating <u>profitably and efficient</u>; shelves
     A           B
   <u>were well stocked</u>, goods were selling rapidly, and the cash register
     C
   <u>was ringing constantly</u>. <u>No error</u>
     D     E

8. Shakespeare's comedies have an advantage <u>over Shaw</u> <u>in that</u> Shakespeare's were
                 A   B
   <u>written primarily</u> to entertain and <u>not to</u> argue for a cause. <u>No error</u>
    C         D       E

9. Any true insomniac <u>is well aware of</u> the futility of <u>such measures as</u> drinking
          A         B
   hot milk, <u>regular hours, deep breathing</u>, counting sheep, and <u>concentrating on</u>
         C             D
   black velvet. <u>No error</u>
       E

Questions 10-15.

DIRECTIONS: In each of the following sentences, some part of the sentence or the entire sentence is underlined. Beneath each sentence you will find five ways of phrasing the underlined part. The first of these repeats the original; the other four are different. If you think the original is better than any of the alternatives, choose answer A; otherwise choose one of the others. In choosing answers, follow the requirements of standard written English; that is, pay attention to grammar, choice of words, sentence construction, and punctuation. Choose the answer that produces the most effective sentence—clear and exact, without awkwardness or ambiguity. Do not make a choice that changes the meaning of the original sentence.

10. The tribe of warriors believed that boys and girls should be <u>reared separate, and, as soon as he was weaned, the boys were taken from their mothers.</u>
   A. reared separate, and, as soon as he was weaned, the boys were taken from their mothers

B. reared separate, and, as soon as he was weaned, a boy was taken from his mother
C. reared separate, and, as soon as he was weaned, the boys were taken from their mothers
D. reared separately, and, as soon as a boy was weaned, they were taken from their mothers
E. reared separately, and, as soon as a boy was weaned, he was taken from his mother

11. <u>Despite Vesta being only the third largest, it is by far the brightest of the known asteroids.</u>
    A. Despite Vesta being only the third largest, it is by far the brightest of the known asteroids.
    B. Vesta, though only the third largest asteroid, is by far the brightest of the known ones.
    C. Being only the third largest, yet Vesta is by far the brightest of the known asteroids.
    D. Vesta, though only the third largest of the known asteroids, is by far the brightest.
    E. Vesta is only the third largest of the asteroids, it being, however, the brightest one.

12. As a result of the discovery of the Dead Sea Scrolls, our understanding of the roots of Christianity <u>has had to be revised considerably.</u>
    A. has had to be revised considerably
    B. have had to be revised considerably
    C. has had to undergo revision to a considerable degree
    D. have had to be subjected to considerable revision
    E. has had to be revised in a considerable way

13. Because <u>it is imminently suitable to</u> dry climates, adobe has been a traditional building material throughout the southwestern states.
    A. it is imminently suitable to
    B. it is eminently suitable for
    C. It is eminently suitable when in
    D. of its eminent suitability with
    E. of being imminently suitable in

14. <u>Martell is more concerned with demonstrating that racial prejudice exists than preventing it from doing harm, which explains</u> why his work is not always highly regarded.
    A. Martell is more concerned with demonstrating that racial prejudice exists than preventing it from doing harm, which explains
    B. Martell is more concerned with demonstrating that racial prejudice exists than with preventing it from doing harm, and this explains
    C. Martell is more concerned with demonstrating that racial prejudice exists than with preventing it from doing harm, an explanation of
    D. Martell's greater concern for demonstrating that racial prejudice exists than preventing it from doing harm—this explains
    E. Martell's greater concern for demonstrating that racial prejudice exists than for preventing it from doing harm explains

15. <u>Throughout this history of the American West there runs a steady commentary on the deception and mistreatment of the Indians.</u>   15.____
   A. Throughout this history of the American West there runs a steady commentary on the deception and mistreatment of the Indians.
   B. There is a steady commentary provided on the deception and mistreatment of the Indians and it runs throughout this history of the American West.
   C. The deception and mistreatment of the Indians provide a steady comment that runs throughout this history of the American West.
   D. Comment on the deception and mistreatment of the Indians is steadily provided and runs throughout this history of the American West.
   E. Running throughout this history of the American West is a steady commentary that is provided on the deception and mistreatment of the Indians.

Questions 16-20.

DIRECTIONS: In each of the following questions you are given a complete sentence to be rephrased according to the directions which follow it. You should rephrase the sentence mentally to save time, although you may make notes in your test book if you wish. Below each sentence and its directions are listed words or phrases that may occur in your revised sentence. When you have thought out a good sentence, look in the choices A through E for the word or entire phrase that is included in your revised sentence, and print the letter of the correct answer in the space at the right. The word or phrase you choose should be the most accurate and most nearly complete of all the choices given, and should be part of a sentence that meets the requirements of standard written English. Of course, a number of different sentences can be obtained if the sentence is revised according to directions, and not all of these possibilities can be included in only five choices. If you should find that you have thought of a sentence that contains none of the words or phrases listed in the choices, you should attempt to rephrase the sentence again so that it includes a word or phrase that is listed. Although the directions may at times require you to change the relationship between parts of the sentence or to make slight changes in meaning in other ways, <u>make only those changes that the directions require</u>; that is, keep the meaning the same, or as nearly the same as the directions permit. If you think that more than one good sentence can be made according to the directions, select the sentence that is most exact, effective, and natural in phrasing and construction.

## EXAMPLES

I. <u>Sentence</u>: Coming to the city as a young man, he found a job as a newspaper reporter.
   <u>Directions</u>: Substitute <u>He came</u> for <u>Coming</u>.
   A. and so he found          B. and found
   C. and there he had found   D. and then finding
   E. and had found

Your rephrased sentence will probably read: "He came to the city as a young man and found a job as a newspaper reporter." This sentence contains the correct answer: <u>B. and found</u>. A sentence which used one of the alternate phrases would <u>change the</u> meaning or <u>intention</u> of the original sentence, would be a <u>poorly written sentence</u>, or would be <u>less effective</u> than another possible revision.

II. <u>Sentence</u>: Owing to her wealth, Sarah had many suitors.
<u>Directions</u>: Begin with <u>Many men courted</u>.
   A. so     B. while     C. although     D. because     E. and

Your rephrased sentence will probably read: "Many men courted Sarah because she was wealthy." This new sentence contains only choice D, which is the correct answer. None of the other choices will fit into an effective, correct sentence that retains the original meaning.

16. The archaeologists could only mark out the burial site, for then winter came.
Begin with <u>Winter came before</u>.
   A. could do nothing more     B. could not do anything
   C. could only do     D. could do something
   E. could do anything more

17. The white reader often receives some insight into the reasons why black men are angry from descriptions by a black writer of the injustice they encounter in a white society.
Begin with <u>A black writer often gives</u>.
   A. when describing     B. by describing
   C. he has described     D. in the descriptions
   E. because of describing

18. The agreement between the university officials and the dissident students provides for student representation on every university committee and on the board of trustees.
Substitute <u>provides that</u> for <u>provides for</u>.
   A. be     B. are     C. would have
   D. would be     E. is to be

19. English Romanticism had its roots in German idealist philosophy, first described in England by Samuel Coleridge.
Begin with <u>Samuel Coleridge was the first in</u>.
   A. in which English     B. and from it English
   C. where English     D. the source of English
   E. the birth of English

20. Four months have passed since his dismissal, during which time Alan has looked for work daily.
Begin with <u>Each day</u>.
   A. will have passed     B. that have passed     C. that passed
   D. were to pass     E. had passed

## KEY (CORRECT ANSWERS)

| | | | |
|---|---|---|---|
| 1. | B | 11. | D |
| 2. | E | 12. | A |
| 3. | D | 13. | B |
| 4. | C | 14. | E |
| 5. | A | 15. | A |
| 6. | B | 16. | E |
| 7. | B | 17. | B |
| 8. | A | 18. | A |
| 9. | C | 19. | D |
| 10. | E | 20. | B |

# PREPARING WRITTEN MATERIAL
# EXAMINATION SECTION
# TEST 1

DIRECTIONS: Each question consists of a sentence which may or may not be an example of good English usage. Examine each sentence, considering grammar, punctuation, spelling, capitalization, and awkwardness. Then choose the correct statement about it from the four choices below it. If the English usage in the sentence given is better than any of the changes suggested in choices B, C, or D, pick choice A. (Do not pick a choice that will change the meaning of the sentence.) *PRINT THE LETTER OF THE CORRECT ANSWER IN THE SPACE AT THE RIGHT.*

1. We attended a staff conference on Wednesday the new safety and fire rules were discussed.  1.____
    A. This is an example of acceptable writing.
    B. The words "safety," "fire," and "rules" should begin with capital letters.
    C. There should be a comma after the word "Wednesday."
    D. There should be a period after the word "Wednesday" and the word "the" should begin with a capital letter.

2. Neither the dictionary or the telephone directory could be found in the office library.  2.____
    A. This is an example of acceptable writing.
    B. The word "or" should be changed to "nor."
    C. The word "library" should be spelled "libery."
    D. The word "neither" should be changed to "either."

3. The report would have been typed correctly if the typist could read the draft.  3.____
    A. This is an example of acceptable writing.
    B. The word "would" should be removed.
    C. The word "have" should be inserted after the word "could."
    D. The word "correctly" should be changed to "correct."

4. The supervisor brought the reports and forms to an employees desk.  4.____
    A. This is an example of acceptable writing.
    B. The word "brought" should be changed to "took."
    C. There should be a comma after the word "reports" and a comma after the word "forms."
    D. The word "employees" should be spelled "employee's."

5. It's important for all the office personnel to submit their vacation schedules on time.  5.____
    A. This is an example of acceptable writing.
    B. The word "It's" should be spelled "Its."
    C. The word "their" should be spelled "they're."
    D. The word "personnel" should be spelled "personal."

6. The report, along with the accompanying documents, were submitted for review.
   A. This is an example of acceptable writing.
   B. The words "were submitted" should be changed to "was submitted."
   C. The word "accompanying" should be spelled "accompaning."
   D. The comma after the word "report" should be taken out.

7. If others must use your files, be certain that they understand how the system works, but insist that you do all the filing and refiling.
   A. This is an example of acceptable writing.
   B. There should be a period after the word "works," and the word "but" should start a new sentence.
   C. The words "filing" and "refiling" should be spelled "fileing" and "refileing."
   D. There should be a comma after the word "but."

8. The appeal was not considered because of its late arrival.
   A. This is an example of acceptable writing.
   B. The word "its" should be changed to "it's."
   C. The word "its" should be changed to "the."
   D. The words "late arrival" should be changed to "arrival late."

9. The letter must be read carefuly to determine under which subject it should be filed.
   A. This is an example of acceptable writing.
   B. The word "under" should be changed to "at."
   C. The word "determine" should be spelled "determin."
   D. The word "carefuly" should be spelled "carefully."

10. He showed potential as an office manager, but he lacked skill in delegating work.
    A. This is an example of acceptable writing.
    B. The word "delegating" should be spelled "delagating."
    C. The word "potential" should be spelled "potencial."
    D. The words "he lacked" should be changed to "was lacking."

# KEY (CORRECT ANSWERS)

| | | | |
|---|---|---|---|
| 1. | D | 6. | B |
| 2. | B | 7. | A |
| 3. | C | 8. | A |
| 4. | D | 9. | D |
| 5. | A | 10. | A |

# TEST 2

DIRECTIONS: Each question consists of a sentence which may or may not be an example of good English usage. Examine each sentence, considering grammar, punctuation, spelling, capitalization, and awkwardness. Then choose the correct statement about it from the four choices below it. If the English usage in the sentence given is better than any of the changes suggested in choices B, C, or D, pick choice A. (Do not pick a choice that will change the meaning of the sentence.) *PRINT THE LETTER OF THE CORRECT ANSWER IN THE SPACE AT THE RIGHT.*

1. The supervisor wants that all staff members report to the office at 9:00 A.M.  1.____
   A. This is an example of acceptable writing.
   B. The word "that" should be removed and the word "to" should be inserted after the word "members."
   C. There should be a comma after the word "wants" and a comma after the word "office."
   D. The word "wants" should be changed to "want" and the word "shall" should be inserted after the word "members."

2. Every morning the clerk opens the office mail and distributes it.  2.____
   A. This is an example of acceptable writing.
   B. The word "opens" should be changed to "open."
   C. The word "mail" should be changed to "letters."
   D. The word "it" should be changed to "them."

3. The secretary typed more fast on a desktop computer than on a laptop computer.  3.____
   A. This is an example of acceptable writing.
   B. The words "more fast" should be changed to "faster."
   C. There should be a comma after the words "desktop computer."
   D. The word "than" should be changed to "then."

4. The new stenographer needed a desk a computer, a chair and a blotter.  4.____
   A. This is an example of acceptable writing.
   B. The word "blotter" should be spelled "blodder."
   C. The word "stenographer" should begin with a capital letter.
   D. There should be a comma after the word "desk."

5. The recruiting officer said, "There are many different goverment jobs available."  5.____
   A. This is an example of acceptable writing.
   B. The word "There" should not be capitalized.
   C. The word "government" should be spelled "government."
   D. The comma after the word "said" should be removed.

6. He can recommend a mechanic whose work is reliable.  6.____
   A. This is an example of acceptable writing.
   B. The word "reliable" should be spelled "relyable."
   C. The word "whose" should be spelled "who's."
   D. The word "mechanic should be spelled "mecanic."

119

7. She typed quickly; like someone who had not a moment to lose.
   A. This is an example of acceptable writing.
   B. The word "not" should be removed.
   C. The semicolon should be changed to a comma.
   D. The word "quickly" should be placed before instead of after the word "typed."

8. She insisted that she had to much work to do.
   A. This is an example of acceptable writing.
   B. The word "insisted" should be spelled "incisted."
   C. The word "to" used in front of "much" should be spelled "too."
   D. The word "do" should be changed to "be done."

9. He excepted praise from his supervisor for a job well done.
   A. This is an example of acceptable writing.
   B. The word "excepted" should be spelled "accepted."
   C. The order of the words "well done" should be changed to "done well."
   D. There should be a comma after the word "supervisor."

10. What appears to be intentional errors in grammar occur several times in the passage.
    A. This is an example of acceptable writing.
    B. The word "occur" should be spelled "occurr."
    C. The word "appears" should be changed to "appear."
    D. The phrase "several times" should be changed to "from time to time."

# KEY (CORRECT ANSWERS)

| | | | |
|---|---|---|---|
| 1. | B | 6. | A |
| 2. | A | 7. | C |
| 3. | B | 8. | C |
| 4. | D | 9. | B |
| 5. | C | 10. | C |

# TEST 3

DIRECTIONS: Each question consists of a sentence which may or may not be an example of good English usage. Examine each sentence, considering grammar, punctuation, spelling, capitalization, and awkwardness. Then choose the correct statement about it from the four choices below it. If the English usage in the sentence given is better than any of the changes suggested in choices B, C, or D, pick choice A. (Do not pick a choice that will change the meaning of the sentence.) *PRINT THE LETTER OF THE CORRECT ANSWER IN THE SPACE AT THE RIGHT.*

1. The clerk could have completed the assignment on time if he knows where these materials were located.
    A. This is an example of acceptable writing.
    B. The word "knows" should be replaced by "had known."
    C. The word "were" should be replaced by "had been."
    D. The words "where these materials were located" should be replaced by "the location of these materials."

2. All employees should be given safety training. Not just those who accidents.
    A. This is an example of acceptable writing.
    B. The period after the word "training" should be changed to a colon.
    C. The period after the word "training" should be changed to a semicolon, and the first letter of the word "Not" should be changed to a small "n."
    D. The period after the word "training" should be changed to a comma, and the first letter of the word "Not" should be changed to a small "n."

3. This proposal is designed to promote employee awareness of the suggestion program, to encourage employee participation in the program, and to increase the number of suggestions submitted.
    A. This is an example of acceptable writing.
    B. The word "proposal" should be spelled "proposal."
    C. The words "to increase the number of suggestions submitted" should be changed to "an increase in the number of suggestions is expected."
    D. The word "promote" should be changed to "enhance" and the word "increase" should be changed to "add to."

4. The introduction of inovative managerial techniques should be preceded by careful analysis of the specific circumstances and conditions in each department.
    A. This is an example of acceptable writing.
    B. The word "technique" should be spelled "techneques."
    C. The word "inovative" should be spelled "innovative."
    D. A comma should be placed after the word "circumstances" and after the word "conditions."

5. This occurrence indicates that such criticism embarrasses him.  5.____
   A. This is an example of acceptable writing.
   B. The word "occurrence" should be spelled "occurence."
   C. The word "criticism" should be spelled "critisism.
   D. The word "embarrasses" should be spelled "embarasses.

## KEY (CORRECT ANSWERS)

1. B
2. D
3. A
4. C
5. A

# PREPARING WRITTEN MATERIAL

# PARAGRAPH REARRANGEMENT
# COMMENTARY

The sentences that follow are in scrambled order. You are to rearrange them in proper order and indicate the letter choice containing the correct answer at the space at the right.

Each group of sentences in this section is actually a paragraph presented in scrambled order. Each sentence in the group has a place in that paragraph; no sentence is to be left out. You are to read each group of sentences and decide upon the best order in which to put the sentences so as to form a well-organized paragraph.

The questions in this section measure the ability to solve a problem when all the facts relevant to its solution are not given.

More specifically, certain positions of responsibility and authority require the employee to discover connection between events sometimes, apparently, unrelated. In order to do this, the employee will find it necessary to correctly infer that unspecified events have probably occurred or are likely to occur. This ability becomes especially important when action must be taken on incomplete information.

Accordingly, these questions require competitors to choose among several suggested alternatives, each of which presents a different sequential arrangement of the events. Competitors must choose the MOST logical of the suggested sequences.

In order to do so, they may be required to draw on general knowledge to infer missing concepts or events that are essential to sequencing the given events. Competitors should be careful to infer only what is essential to the sequence. The plausibility of the wrong alternatives will always require the inclusion of unlikely events or of additional chains of events which are NOT essential to sequencing the given events.

It's very important to remember that you are looking for the best of the four possible choices, and that the best choice of all may not even be one of the answers you're given to choose from.

There is no one right way to solve these problems. Many people have found it helpful to first write out the order of the sentences, as they would have arranged them, on their scrap paper before looking at the possible answers. If their optimum answer is there, this can save them some time. If it isn't, this method can still give insight into solving the problem. Others find it most helpful to just go through each of the possible choices, contrasting each as they go along. You should use whatever method feels comfortable and works for you.

While most of these types of questions are not that difficult, we've added a higher percentage of the difficult type, just to give you more practice. Usually there are only one or two questions on this section that contain such subtle distinctions that you're unable to answer confidently. And you then may find yourself stuck deciding between two possible choices, neither of which you're sure about.

# PREPARING WRITTEN MATERIAL
# PARAGRAPH REARRANGEMENT
## EXAMINATION SECTION
## TEST 1

DIRECTIONS: The following groups of sentences need to be arranged in an order that makes sense. Select the letter preceding the sequence that represents the best sentence order. *PRINT THE LETTER OF THE CORRECT ANSWER IN THE SPACE AT THE RIGHT.*

1.  I. The ostrich egg shell's legendary toughness makes it an excellent substitute for certain types of dishes or dinnerware, and in parts of Africa ostrich shells are cut and decorated for use as containers for water.
    II. Since prehistoric times, people have used the enormous egg of the ostrich as a part of their diet, a practice which has required much patience and hard work—to hard boil an ostrich egg takes about four hours.
    III. Opening the egg's shell, which is rock hard and nearly an inch thick, requires heavy tools, such as a saw or chisel; from inside, a baby ostrich must use a hornlike projection on its beak as a miniature pick-axe to escape from the egg.
    IV. The offspring of all higher-order animals originate from single egg cells that are carried by mothers, and most of these eggs are relatively small, often microscopic.
    V. The egg of the African ostrich, however, weighs a massive thirty pounds, making it the largest single cell on earth, and a common object of human curiosity and wonder.

    The BEST order is:
    A. V, IV, I, II, III    B. I, IV, V, III, II    C. IV, II, III, V, I    D. IV, V, II, III, I

    1.____

2.  I. Typically only a few feet high on the open sea, individual tsunami have been known to circle the entire globe two or three times if their progress is not interrupted, but are not usually dangerous until they approach the shallow water that surrounds land masses.
    II. Some of the most terrifying and damaging hazards caused by earthquakes are tsunami, which were once called "tidal waves"—a poorly chosen name, since these waves have nothing to do with tides.
    III. Then a wave, slowed by the sudden drag on the lower part of its moving water column, will pile upon itself, sometimes reaching a height of over 100 feet.
    IV. Tsunami (Japanese for "great harbor wave") are seismic waves that are caused by earthquakes near oceanic trenches, and once triggered, can travel up to 600 miles an hour on the open ocean.
    V. A land-shoaling tsunami is capable of extraordinary destruction; some tsunami have deposited large boats miles inland, washed out two-foot-thick seawalls, and scattered locomotive trains over long distances.

    The BEST order is:
    A. IV, I, III, II, V    B. I, III, IV, II, V    C. V, I, III, II, IV    D. II, IV, I, III, V

    2.____

125

3.
   I. Soon, by the 1940s, jazz was the most popular type of music among American intellectuals and college students.
   II. In the early days of jazz, it was considered "lowdown" music, or music that was played only in rough, disreputable bars and taverns.
   III. However, jazz didn't take too long to develop from early ragtime melodies into more complex, sophisticated forms, such as Charlie Parker's "bebop" style of jazz.
   IV. After charismatic band leaders such as Duke Ellington and Count Basie brought jazz to a larger audience, and jazz continued to evolve into more complicated forms, white audiences began to accept and even to enjoy the new American art form.
   V. Many white Americans, who then dictated the tastes of society, were wary of music that was played almost exclusively in black clubs in the poorer sections of cities and towns.

   The BEST order is:
   A. V, IV, III, II, I    B. II, V, III, IV, I    C. IV, V, III, I, II    D. I, II, IV, III, V

4.
   I. Then, hanging in a windless place, the magnetized end of the needle would always point to the south.
   II. The needle could then be balanced on the rim of a cup, or the edge of a fingernail, but this balancing act was hard to maintain, and the needle often fell off.
   III. Other needles would point to the north, and it was important for any traveler finding his way with a compass to remember which kind of magnetized needle he was carrying.
   IV. To make some of the earliest compasses in recorded history, ancient Chinese "magicians" would rub a needle with a piece of magnetized iron called a lodestone.
   V. A more effective method of keeping the needle free to swing with its magnetic pull was to attach a strand of silk to the center of the needle with a tiny piece of wax.

   The BEST order is:
   A. IV, II, V, I, III    B. IV, III, V, II, I    C. IV, V, II, I, III    D. IV, I, III, V, II

5.
   I. The now-famous first mate of the *H.M.S. Bounty*, Fletcher Christian, founded one of the world's most peculiar civilizations in 1790.
   II. The men knew they had just committed a crime for which they could be hanged, so they set sail for Pitcairn, a remote, abandoned island in the far eastern region of the Polynesian archipelago, accompanied by twelve Polynesian women and six men.
   III. In a mutiny that has become legendary, Christian and the others forced Captain Bligh into a lifeboat and set him adrift off the coast of Tonga in April of 1789.
   IV. In early 1790, the *Bounty* landed at Pitcairn Island, where the men lived out the rest of their lives and founded an isolated community which to this day includes direct descendants of Christian and the other Crewmen.

V. The *Bounty*, commanded by Captain William Bligh, was in the middle of a global voyage, and Christian and his shipmates had come to the conclusion that Bligh was a reckless madman who would lead them to their deaths unless they took the ship from him.

The BEST order is:
  A. IV, V, III, II, I
  B. I, III, V, II, IV
  C. I, V, III, II, IV
  D. III, I, V, IV, II

6.  I. But once the vines had been led to make orchids, the flowers had to be carefully hand-pollinated, because unpollinated orchids usually lasted less than a day, wilting and dropping off the vine before it had even become dark.
    II. The Totonac farmers discovered that looping a vine back around once it reached a five-foot height on its host tree would cause the vine to flower.
    III. Though they knew how to process the fruit pods and extract vanilla's flavoring agent, the Totonacs also knew that a wild vanilla vine did not produce abundant flowers or fruit.
    IV. Wild vines climbed along the trunks and canopies of trees, and this constant upward growth diverted most of the vine's energy to making leaves instead of the orchid flowers that once pollinated, would produce the flavorful pods.
    V. Hundreds of years before vanilla became a prized food flavoring in Europe and the Western World, the Totonac Indians of the Mexican Gulf Coast were skilled cultivators of the vanilla vine, whose fruit they literally worshipped as a goddess.

The BEST order is:
  A. II, III, IV, I, V
  B. II, IV, III, I, V
  C. V, III, IV, II, I
  D. III, IV, I, II, V

7.  I. Once airborne, the spider is at the mercy of the air currents—usually the spider takes a brief journey, traveling close to the ground, but some have been found in air samples collected as high as 10,000 feet, or been reported landing on ships far out at sea.
    II. Once a young spider has hatched, it must leave the environment into which it was born as quickly as possible, in order to avoid competing with its hundreds of brothers and sisters for food.
    III. The silk rises into warm air currents, and as soon as the pull feels adequate the spider lets go and drifts up into the air, suspended from the silk strand in the same way that a person might parasail.
    IV. To help young spiders do this, many species have adapted a practice known as "aerial dispersal," or, in common speech, "ballooning."
    V. A spider that wants to leave its surroundings quickly will climb to the top of a grass system or twig, face into the wind, and aim its back end into the air, releasing a long stream of silk from the glands near the tip of its abdomen.

The BEST order is:
  A. V, IV, II, III, I
  B. V, II, IV, I, III
  C. II, V, IV, III, I
  D. II, IV, V, III, I

8.  I. For about a year, Tycho worked at a castle in Prague with a scientist named Johannes Kepler, but their association was cut short by another argument that drove Kepler out of the castle, to later develop, on his own, the theory of planetary orbits.
    II. Tycho found life without a nose embarrassing, so he made a new nose for himself out of silver, which reportedly remained glued to his face for the rest of his life.
    III. Tycho Brahe, the 17th-century Danish astronomer, is today more famous for his odd and arrogant personality than for any contribution he has made to our knowledge of the stars and planets.
    IV. Early in his career, as a student at Rostock University, Tycho got into an argument with another student about who was the better mathematician, and the two became so angry that the argument turned into a sword fight, during which Tycho's nose was sliced off.
    V. Later in his life, Tycho's arrogance may have kept him from playing a part in one of the greatest astronomical discoveries in history: the elliptical orbits of the solar system's planets.
    The BEST order is:
    A. I, IV, II, III, V     B. IV, II, III, V, I     C. IV, II, I, III, V     D. III, IV, II, V, I

9.  I. The processionaries are so used to this routine that if a person picks up the end of a silk line and brings it back to the origin—creating a closed circle—the caterpillars may travel around and around for days, sometimes starving or freezing, without changing course.
    II. Rather than relying on sight or sound, the other caterpillars, who are lined up end-to-end behind the leader, travel to and from their nests by walking on this silk line, and each will reinforce it by laying down its own marking line as it passes over.
    III. In order to insure the safety of individuals, the processionary caterpillar nests in a tree with dozens of other caterpillars, and at night, when it is safest, they all leave together in search of food.
    IV. The processionary caterpillar of the European continent is a perfect illustration of how much some inspect species rely on instinct in their daily routines.
    V. As they leave their nests, the processionaries form a single-file line behind a leader who spins and lays out a silk line to mark the chosen path.
    The BEST order is:
    A. IV, III, V, II, I     B. III, V, IV, II, I     C. III, V, II, I, IV     D. IV, V, III, I, II

10. I. Often, the child is also given a handcrafted walker or push cart, to provide support for its first upright explorations.
    II. In traditional Indian families, a child's first steps are celebrated as a ceremonial event, rooted in ancient myth.
    III. These carts are often intricately designed to resemble the chariot of Krishna, an important figure in Indian mythology.
    IV. The sound of these anklet bells is intended to mimic the footsteps of the legendary child Rama, who is celebrated in devotional songs throughout India.

V. When the child's parents see that the child is ready to begin walking, they will fit it with specially designed ankle bracelets, adorned with gently ringing bells.

The BEST order is:
A. II, III, IV, I, V   B. II, V, III, I, IV   C. V, IV, I, III, II   D. V, III, II, I, IV

11. I. The settlers planted Osage oranges all across Middle America, and today long lines and rectangles of Osage orange trees can still be seen on the prairies, running along the former boundaries of farms that no longer exist.
    II. After trying sod walls and water-filled ditches with no success, American farmers began to look for a plant that was adaptable to prairie weather, and that could be trimmed into a hedge that was "pig-tight, horse-high, and bull-strong."
    III. The tree, so named because it bore a large (but inedible) fruit the size of an orange, was among the sturdiest and hardiest of American trees, and was prized among Native Americans for the strength and flexibility of bows which were made from its wood.
    IV. The first people to practice agriculture on the American flatlands were faced with an important problem: what would they use to fence their land in a place that was almost entirely without trees or rocks?
    V. Finally, an Illinois farmer brought the settlers a tree that was native to the land between the Red and Arkansas rivers, a tree called the Osage orange.

    The BEST order is:
    A. II, I, V, III, IV   B. I, II, III, IV, V   C. IV, II, V, III, I   D. IV, II, I, III, V

12. I. After about ten minutes of such spirited and complicated activity, the head dancer is free to make up his or her own movements while maintaining the interest of the New Year's crowd.
    II. The dancer will then perform a series of leg kicks, while at the same time operating the lion's mouth with his own hand and moving the ears and eyes by means of a string which is attached to the dancer's own mouth.
    III. The most difficult role of this dance belongs to the one who controls the lion's head; this person must lead all the other "parts" of the lion through the choreographed segments of the dance.
    IV. The head dancer begins with a complex series of steps. alternately stepping forward with the head raised, and then retreating a few steps while lowering the head, a movement that is intended to create the impression that the lion is keeping a watchful eye for anything evil.
    V. When performing a traditional Chinese New Year's lion dance, several performers must fit themselves inside a large lion costume and work together to enact different parts of the dance.

    The BEST order is:
    A. V, III, IV, II, I   B. III, IV, II, V, I   C. III, I, V, IV, II   D. IV, II, III, V, I

13.  I. For many years the shell of the chambered nautilus was treasured in Europe for its beauty and intricacy, but collectors were unaware that they were in possession of the structure that marked a "missing link" in the evolution of marine mollusks.
II. The nautilus, however, evolved a series of enclosed chambers in its shell, and invented a new use for the structure: the shell began to serve as a buoyancy device.
III. Equipped with this new flotation device, the nautilus did not need the single, muscular foot of its predecessors, but instead developed flaps, tentacles, and a gentle form of jet propulsion that transformed it into the first mollusk able to take command of its own density and explore a three-dimensional world.
IV. By pumping and adjusting air pressure into the chambers, the nautilus could spend the day resting on the bottom, and then rise toward the surface at night in search of food.
V. The nautilus shell looks like a large snail shell, similar to those of its ancestors, who used their shells as protective coverings while they were anchored to the sea floor.
The BEST order is:
A. V, II, IV, I, III   B. V, I, II, III, IV   C. I, II, V, III, IV   D. I, V, II, IV, III

13.____

14.  I. While France and England battled for control of the region, the Acadiens prospered on the fertile farmland, which was finally secured by England in 1713.
II. Early in the 17th century, settlers from Western France founded a colony called Acadie in what is now the Canadian province of Nova Scotia.
III. At this time, English officials feared the presence of spies among the Acadiens who might be loyal to their French homeland, and the Acadiens were deported to spots along the Atlantic and Caribbean shores of America.
IV. The French settlers remained on this land, under English rule, for around forty years, until the beginning of the French and Indian War, another conflict between France and England.
V. As the Acadien refugees drifted toward a final home in Southern Louisiana, neighbors shortened their name to "Cadien," and finally "Cajun," the name which the descendants of early Acadiens still call themselves.
The BEST order is:
A. I, IV, II, III, V   B. II, I, III, V, IV   C. II, I, IV, III, V   D. V, II, III, IV, I

14.____

15.  I. Traditional households in the Eastern and Western regions of Africa serve two meals a day—one at around noon, and the other in the evening.
II. The starch is then used in the way that Americans might use a spoon, to scoop up a portion of the main dish on the person's plate.
III. The reason for the starch's inclusion in every meal has to do with taste as well as nutrition; African food can be very spicy, and the starch is known to cool the burning effect of the main dish.
IV. When serving these meals, the main dish is usually served on individual plates, and the starch is served on a communal plate, from which diners break off a piece of bread or scoop rice or fufu in their fingers.

15.____

V. The typical meals usually consist of a thick stew or soup as the main course, and an accompanying starch—either bread, rice, or *fufu*, a starchy grain paste similar in consistency to mashed potatoes.
The BEST order is:
A. V, II, III, IV, I   B. V, I, IV, III, II   C. I, IV, V, III, II   D. I, V, IV, II, III

16. I. In the early days of the American Midwest, Indiana settlers sometimes came together to hold an event called an apple peeling, where neighboring settlers gathered at the homestead of a host family to help prepare the hosts' apple crop for cooking, canning, and making apple butter.
    II. At the beginning of the event, each peeler sat down in front of a ten- or twenty-gallon stone jar and was given a crock of apples and a paring knife.
    III. Once a peeler had finished with a crock, another was placed next to him; if the peeler was an unmarried man, he kept a strict count of the number of apples he had peeled, because the winner was allowed to kiss the girl of his choice.
    IV. The peeling usually ended by 9:30 in the evening, when the neighbors gathered in the host family's parlor for a dance social.
    V. The apples were peeled, cored, and quartered, and then placed into the jar.
    The BEST order is:
    A. I, V, III, IV, II   B. II, V, III, IV, I   C. I, II, V, III, IV   D. II, I, V, IV, III

16.____

17. I. If your pet turtle is a land turtle and is native to temperate climates, it will stop eating some time in October, which should be your cue to prepare the turtle for hibernation.
    II. The box should then be covered with a wire screen, which will protect the turtle from any rodents or predators that might want to take advantage of a motionless and helpless animal.
    III. When your turtle hasn't eaten for a while and appears ready to hibernate, it should be moved to its winter quarters, most likely a cellar or garage, where the temperature should range between 40° and 45°F.
    IV. Instead of feeding the turtle, you should bathe it every day in warm water, to encourage the turtle to empty its intestines in preparation for its long winter sleep.
    V. Here the turtle should be placed in a well-ventilated box whose bottom is covered with a moisture-absorbing layer of clay beads, and then filled three-fourths full with almost dry peat moss or wood chips, into which the turtle will burrow and sleep for several months.
    The BEST order is:
    A. I, IV, III, V, II   B. III, IV, II, V, I   C. III, II, IV, I, V   D. IV, V, II, III, I

17.____

18. I. Once he has reached the nest, the hunter uses two sturdy bamboo poles like huge chopsticks to pull the next away from the mountainside, into a large basket that will be lowered to people waiting below.
    II. The world's largest honeybees colonize the Nealese mountainsides, building honeycombs as large as a person on sheer rock faces that are often hundreds of feet high.

18.____

III. In the remote mountain country of Nepal, a small band of "honey hunters" carry out a tradition so ancient that 10,000 year-old drawings of the practice have been found in the caves of Nepal.

IV. To harvest the honey and beeswax from these combs, a honey hunter climbs above the nests, lowers a long bamboo-fiber ladder over the cliff, and then climbs down.

V. Throughout this dangerous practice, the hunter is stung repeatedly, and only the veterans, with skin that has been toughened over the years, are able to return from a hunt without the painful swelling caused by stings.

The BEST order is:

A. II, IV, III, V, I     B. II, IV, I, V, III     C. V, III, II, IV, I     D. III, II, IV, I, V

19. I. After the Romans left Britain, there were relentless attacks on the islands from the barbarian tribes of northern Germany—the Angles, Saxons, and Jutes.

II. As the empire weakened, Roman soldiers withdrew from Britain, leaving behind a country that continued to practice the Christian religion that had been introduced by the Romans.

III. Early Latin writings tell of a Christian warrior named Arturius (Arthur, in English) who led the British citizens to defeat these barbarian invades, and brought an extended period of peace to the lands of Britain.

IV. Long ago, the British Isles were part of the far-flung Roman Empire that extended across most of Europe and into Africa and Asia.

V. The romantic legend of King Arthur and his knights of the Round Table, one of the most popular and widespread stories of all time, appears to have some foundation in history.

The BEST order is:

A. V, IV, III, II, I     B. V, IV, II, I, III     C. IV, V, II, III, I     D. IV, III, II, I, V

20. I. The cylinder was allowed to cool until it could stand on its own, and then it was cut from the tube and split down the side with a single straight cut.

II. Nineteenth-century glassmakers, who had not yet discovered the glazier's modern techniques for making panes of glass, had to create a method for converting their blown gas into flat sheets.

III. The bubble was then pierced at the end to make a hole that opened up while the glassmaker gently spun it, creating a cylinder of glass.

IV. Turned on its side and laid on a conveyor belt, the cylinder was strengthened, or tempered, by being heated again and cooled very slowly, eventually flattening out into a single rectangular of glass.

V. To do this, the glassmaker dipped the end of a long tube into melted glass and blew into the other end of the tube, creating an expanding bubble of glass.

The BEST order is:

A. II, V, III, IV, I     B. II, IV, V, III, I     C. III, V, II, IV, I     D. III, I, IV, V, II

21.  I. The splints are almost always hidden, but horses are occasionally born whose splinted toes project from the leg on either side, just above the hoof.
    II. The second and fourth toes remained, but shrank to thin splints of bone that fused invisibly to the horse's leg bone.
    III. Horses are unique among mammals, having evolved feet that each end in what is essentially a single toe, capped by a large, sturdy hoof.
    IV. Julius Caesar, an emperor of ancient Rome, was said to have owned one of these three-toed horses, and considered it so special that he would not permit anyone else to ride it.
    V. Though the horse's earlier ancestors possessed the traditional mammalian set of five toes on each foot, the horse has retained only its third toe; its first and fifth toes disappeared completely as the horse evolved.

    The BEST order is:
    A. III, V, II, I, IV     B. V, III, II, IV, I     C. III, II, V, I, IV     D. V, II, III, I, IV

22.  I. The new building materials—some of which are twenty feet long, and weigh nearly six tons—were transported to Pohnpei on rafts, and were brought into their present position by using hibiscus fiber ropes and leverage to move the stone columns upward along the inclined trunks of coconut palm trees.
    II. The ancestors built great fires to heat the stone, and then poured cool seawater on the columns, which caused the stone to contract and split along natural fracture lines.
    III. The now-abandoned enclave of Nan Madol, a group of 92 man-made islands off the shore of the Micronesian island of Pohnpei, is estimated to have been built around the year 500 A.D.
    IV. The islanders say their ancestors quarried stone columns from a nearby island, where large basalt columns were formed by the cooling of molten lava.
    V. The structures of Nan Madol are remarkable for the sheer size of some of the stone "longs" or columns that were used to create the walls of the offshore community, and today anthropologists can only rely on the information of existing local people for clues about how Nan Madol was built.

    The BEST order is:
    A. V, IV, III, II, I     B. V, III, I, IV, II     C. III, V, IV, II, I     D. III, I, IV, II, V

23.  I. One of the most easily manipulated substances on earth, glass can be made into ceramic tiles that are composed of over 90% air.
    II. NASA's space shuttles are the first spacecraft ever designed to leave and re-enter the earth's atmosphere while remaining intact.
    III. These ceramic tiles are such effective insulators that when a tile emerges from the oven in which it was fired, it can be held safely in a person's hand by the edges while its interior still glows at a temperature well over 2000°F.
    IV. Eventually, the engineers were led to a material that is as old as our most ancient civilization.
    V. Because the temperature during atmospheric re-entry is so incredibly hot, it took NASA's engineers some time to find a substance capable of protecting the shuttles.

The BEST order is:
A. V, II, I, II, IV  B. II, V, IV, I, III  C. II, III, I, IV, V  D. V, IV, III, I, II

24. 
I. The secret to teaching any parakeet to talk is patience, and the understanding that when a bird talks," it is simply imitating what it hears, rather than putting ideas into words.
II. You should stay just out of sight of the bird and repeat the phrase you want it to learn, for at least fifteen minutes every morning and evening.
III. It is important to leave the bird without any words of encouragement or farewell; otherwise it might combine stray remarks or phrases, such as "Good night," with the phrase you are trying to teach it.
IV. For this reason, to train your bird to imitate your words you should keep it free of any distractions, especially other noises, while you are giving it "lesson."
V. After your repetition, you should quietly leave the bird alone for a while, to think over what it has just heard.

The BEST order is:
A. I, IV, II, V, III  B. I, II, IV, III, V  C. III, II, I, V, IV  D. III, I, V, IV, II

25.
I. As a school approaches, fishermen from neighboring communities join their fishing boats together as a fleet, and string their gill nets together to make a huge fence that is held up by cork floats.
II. At a signal from the party leaders, or *nakura*, the family members pound the sides of the boats or beat the water with long poles, creating a sudden and deafening noise.
III. The fishermen work together to drag the trap into a half-circle that may reach 300 yards in diameter, and then the families move their boats to form the other half of the circle around the school of fish.
IV. The school of fish flee from the commotion into the awaiting trap, where a final wall of net is thrown over the open end of the half-circle, securing the day's haul.
V. Indonesian people from the area around the Sulu islands live on the sea, in floating villages made of lashed-together or stilted homes, and make much of their living by fishing their home waters for migrating schools of snapper, scad, and other fish.

The BEST order is:
A. I, V, III, IV, II  B. I, II, IV, III, V  C. V, I, II, III, IV  D. V, I, III, II, IV

## KEY (CORRECT ANSWERS)

| | | | |
|---|---|---|---|
| 1. | D | 11. | C |
| 2. | D | 12. | A |
| 3. | B | 13. | D |
| 4. | A | 14. | C |
| 5. | C | 15. | D |
| 6. | C | 16. | C |
| 7. | D | 17. | A |
| 8. | D | 18. | D |
| 9. | A | 19. | B |
| 10. | B | 20. | A |

21. A
22. C
23. B
24. A
25. D

# BASIC FUNDAMENTALS OF WRITTEN COMMUNICATION

| CONTENTS | Page |
|---|---|
| INSTRUCTIONAL OBJECTIVES | 1 |
| CONTENT | 1 |
|   Introduction | 1 |
| 1. Business Writing | 1 |
|     Letters | |
|       Selet the letter type | |
|       Select the Right Format | |
|       Know the Letter Elements | |
|       Be Breef | |
|       Use Concrete Nouns | |
|       Use Active Verbs | |
|       Use a Natural Tone | |
|     Forms | 4 |
|     Memoranda | 5 |
|     Minutes of meetings | 5 |
|     Short Reports | 6 |
|     News Releases | 8 |
| 2. Reporting on a Topic | 9 |
|     Preparation for the Report | 9 |
|       What is the Purpose of the Report? | |
|       What Questions Should it Answer? | |
|       Where Can the Relevant information be obtained? | |
|     The Text of the Report | 10 |
|       What Are the Answers to the Questions? | |
|       Organizing the Report | |
|     The Writer's Responsibilities | 11 |
|     Conclusions and Recommendations | 11 |
| 3. Persuasive Writing | 11 |
|     General Guidelines for Writing | 11 |
|       Persuasively | |
|       Know the Source Credibility | |
|       Avoid Overemotional Appeal | |
|       Consider the Other Man's Point of wiew | |
|     Interpersonal Communications | 12 |
|       Conditions of Persuading | |
|       The Persuassion campain | |
| 4. Instructional Writing | 13 |
|     Advances Organizers | |
|     Practice | |
|     Errorless Learning | |
|     Feedback | |
| STUDENT LEARNING ACTIVITIES | 16 |
| TEACHERS MANAGEMENT ACTIVTIES | 17 |
| EVALUATION QUESTIONS | 19 |

# BASIC FUNDAMENTALS OF WRITTEN COMMUNICATION

INSTRUCTIONAL OBJECTIVES
1. Ability to write legibly.
2. Ability to fill out forms and applications correctly.
3. Ability to take messages and notes accurately.
4. Ability to write letters effectively.
5. Ability to write directions and instructions clearly.
6. Ability to outline written and spoken information.
7. Ability to persuade or teach others through written communication.
8. Ability to write effective overviews and summaries.
9. Ability to make smooth transitions within written communications.
10. Ability to use language forms appropriate for the reader.
11. Ability to prepare effective informational reports.

CONTENT

INTRODUCTION

Public-service employees are required to prepare written communications for a variety of purposes. Written communication is a fundamental tool, not only for the public-service occupations, but throughout the world of work. Many public-service occupations require written communication with ordinary citizens of diverse backgrounds, so the trainee should develop the ability to write in simple, nontechnical language that the ordinary citizen will understand.

This unit is designed to develop the student's ability to communicate effectively in writing for a number of different purposes and in a number of different formats. Whatever the particular purpose or format, how-- ever, effective writing will require the writer:

- to have a clear idea of his purpose and his audience;
- to organize his thoughts and information in an orderly way;
- to express himself concisely, accurately, and concretely;
- to report relevant facts;
- to explain and summarize ideas clearly; and
- to evaluate the effectiveness of his communication.

1. BUSINESS WRITING
   Several forms of written communication tend to recur frequently in most public-service agencies, including:
   - letters
   - forms
   - memoranda
   - minutes of meetings
   - short reports
   - telegrams and cables
   - news releases
   - and many others

The public-service employee should be familiar with the principles of writing in these forms, and should be able to apply them in preparing effective communications.

Letters

Every letter sent from a public-service agency should be considered an ambassador of goodwill. The impression it creates may mean the difference between favorable public attitudes or unfavorable ones. It may mean the difference between creating a friend or an enemy for the agency. Every public-service employee has a responsibility to serve the public effectively and to provide services in an efficient and courteous manner. The letters an agency sends out reflect its attitudes toward the public.

The impression a letter creates depends upon both its appearance and its tone. A letter which shows erasures and pen written corrections gives an impression that the sending agency is slovenly. Similarly, a rude or impersonal letter creates the impression that the agency is insensitive or unfeeling. In preparing letters, the employee should apply principles of style and tone which will serve to create the most favorable impression.

*Select the Letter Type*. The two most common types of business letters are letters of inquiry and letters of response - that is, "asking" letters and "answering" letters. Whichever type of letter the employee is asked to write, the following guidelines will simplify the task and help to achieve a style and tone which will create a favorable impression on the reader.

*Select the Right Format*. Several styles of letter format are in common use today, including:

- the indented format,
- the block format, and
- the semi-block format.

Modified forms of these are also in use in some offices. The student should become familiar with the formats preferred for usage in his office, and be able to use whichever form the employer requests.

*Know the Letter Elements*. Every letter includes certain basic elements, such as:

- the letterhead, which identifies the name and address of the sender.
- the date on which the letter was transmitted.
- the inside address, with the name, street, city, and state of the addressee.
- the salutation, greeting the addressee.
- the body, containing the message.
- the complimentary close, the "good-bye" of the business letter.
- the signature, handwritten by the sender.
- the typed signature, the typewritten name and title of the sender.

In addition, several other elements are occasionally found in business letters:

- the *attention line,* directing the letter to the attention of a particular individual or his representative.
- the *subject line,* informing the reader at a glance of the subject of the letter.

- the *enclosure notation,* noting items enclosed with the letter.
- the *copy notation,* listing other persons who receive copies of the letter.
- the *postscript,* an afterthought sometimes (but not normally) added following the last typed line of the letter.

<u>Be *Brief.*</u> Use only the words which help to say what is needed in a clear and straightforward manner. Do not repeat information already known to the reader, or contained elsewhere in the letter. Likewise, do not repeat information contained in the letter being answered. Rather than repeat the content of a previous letter, one can say something like, "Please refer to our letter dated March 5:"

An employee can shorten his letters by using single words that serve the same function as longer phrases. Many commonly used phrases can be replaced by single words. For example,

| Phrase | Single word |
|---|---|
| in order to | to |
| in reference to in | about |
| the amount of | for, of |
| in a number of cases | some |
| in view of | because |
| with regard to | about, in |

Similarly, avoid the use of adjectives and nouns that are formed from verbs. If the root verbs are used instead, the writing will be more concise and more vivid. For example,

| Noun form | Verb form |
|---|---|
| We made an adjustment on our books | We adjusted our books |
| We are sorry we cannot make a replacement of | We are sorry we cannot replace |
| Please make a correction in our order | Please correct our order |

Be on the lookout for unnecessary adjectives and adverbs which tend to clutter letters without adding information or improving style. Such unnecessary words tend to distract the reader and make it more difficult for him to grasp the main points. Observe how the superfluous words, italicized in the following example, obscure the meaning: "You may be *very much* disappointed to learn that the *excessively large* demand for our *highly popular recent* publication, 'Your Income Taxes,' has led to an *unexpected* shortage of this *attractive* publication and we *sadly* expect they will not be replenished until *quite* late this year."

Summarizing, then, a *good letter is simple and clear, with short, simple words, sentences, and paragraphs. Related parts* of *sentences and paragraphs are kept together and placed in an order which makes it easy for the reader to follow the main thoughts.*

*Be Natural.* Whenever possible, use a human touch. Use names and personal pronouns to let the reader know the letter was written by a person, not an institution. Instead of saying, "It is the policy of this agency to contact its clients once each year to confirm their status," try this: "Our policy, Mr. Jones, is to confirm your status once each year."

*Use Concrete Nouns.* Avoid using abstract words and generalizations. Use names of objects, places, and persons rather than abstractions.

*Use Active verbs.* The passive voice gives a motionless, weak tone to most writing. Instead of "The minutes were taken by Mrs. Smith," say, "Mrs. Smith took the minutes." Instead of "The plans were prepared by the banquet committee," say, "The banquet committee prepared the plans."

*Use a Natural Tone.* Many people tend to become hard, cold, and unnatural the moment they write a letter. *Communicating by letter should have the same natural tone of conversation used in everyday speech.* One way to achieve a natural and personal tone in the majority of letters is through the use of personal pronouns. Instead of saying, "Referring to your letter of March 5, reporting the non-receipt of goods ordered last February 15, please be advised that the goods were shipped as requested," say, "I am sorry to hear that you failed to receive the items you ordered last February 15. We shipped them the same day we received your letter."

## Forms

In most businesses and public service agencies, repetitive work is simplified by the use of *forms*. Forms exist for nearly every purpose imaginable: for ordering supplies, preparing invoices, applying for jobs, applying for insurance, paying taxes, recording inventories, and so on. While the forms encountered in different agencies may differ widely, several principles should be applied in completing any form:

- *Legibility.* Entries on forms should be clear and legible. Print or type wherever possible. When space provided is insufficient, attach a supplementary sheet to the form.

- *Completeness.* Make an entry in every space provided on the form. If a particular space does not apply to the applicant, enter there the term "N/A" (for "not applicable"). The reader of the completed form will then know that the applicant did not simply overlook that space.

- *Conciseness.* Forms are intended to elicit a maximum amount of information in the least possible space. When completing a form, it is usually not necessary to write complete sentences. Provide the necessary information in the least possible words.

- *Accuracy.* Be sure the information provided on the form is accurate. If the entry is a number, such as a social security number or an address, double-check the correctness of the number. Be sure of the spelling of names, No one appreciates receiving a communication in which his name is misspelled.

## Memoranda

The written communications passing between offices or departments are usually transmitted in a form known as *"interoffice memorandum."* The headings most often used on such "memos" are:

- TO:         identifying the addressee,
- FROM:    identifying the sender or the originating office,
- SUBJECT: identifying briefly the subject of the memo,
- DATE:    identifying the date the memo was prepared.

Larger agencies may also use headings such as FILE or REFERENCE NO. to aid in filing and retrieving memoranda.

In writing a memo, many of the same rules for letter-writing may be applied. Both the appearance and tone of the memo should create a pleasing impression. The format should be neat and follow the standards set by the originating office. The tone should be friendly, courteous, and considerate. The language should be clear, concise, and complete.

Memos usually dispense with salutations, complimentary closings, and signatures of the writers. In most other respects, however, the memorandum will follow the rules of good letter-writing.

## Minutes of Meetings

Most formal public-service organization conduct meetings from time to time at which group decisions are made about agency policies, procedures, and work assignments. The records of such meetings are called *minutes*.

Minutes should be written as clearly and simply as possible, summarizing only the essential facts and decisions made at the meeting. While some issue may have been discussed at great length, only the final decision or resolution made of it should be recorded in the minutes. Information of this sort is usually included:

- Time and place of the call to order,
- Presiding officer and secretary,
- Voting members present (with names, if a small organization),

- Approval and corrections of previous minutes,
- Urgent business,
- Old business,
- New business,
- Time of adjournment,
- Signature of recorder.

Minutes should be written in a factual and objective style. The opinions of the recorder should not be in evidence. Every item of business coming up before a meeting should be included in the minutes, together with its disposition. For example:

- "M/S/P (Moved, seconded, passed) that Mr. Thomas Jones take responsibility for rewriting the personnel procedures manual."
- "Discussion of the summer vacation schedule was tabled until the next meeting."
- "M/S/P, a resolution that no client of the agency should be kept waiting more than 20 minutes for an interview."

Note that considerable discussion may have surrounded each of the above items in the minutes, but that only the topic and its resolution are recorded.

### Short Reports

The public-service employee often is called upon to prepare a short report gathering and interpreting information on a single topic. Reports of this kind are sometimes prepared so that all the relevant information may be assembled in one place to aid the organization in making certain decisions. Such reports may be read primarily by the staff of the organization or by others closely related to the decision-making process.

Reports may be prepared at other times for distribution to the public or to other agencies and institutions. These reports may serve the purpose of informing public opinion or persuading others on matters of public policy.

Whatever the purpose of the short report, its physical appearance and style of presentation should be designed to create a favorable impression on the reader. Even if the report is distributed only within the writer's own unit, an attractive, clear, thorough report will reflect the writer's dedication to his assignment and the pride he takes in his work.

Some guidelines which will assist the trainee in preparation of effective short reports include use of the following:

- A good quality paper;
- Wide and even margins, allowing binding room;

- An accepted standard style of typing;
- A title page;
- A table of contents (for more lengthy reports only);
- A graphic numbering or outlining system, if needed for clarity;
- Graphics and photos to clarify meaning when useful;
- Footnotes, used sparingly, and only when they contribute to the report;
- A bibliography of sources, using a standard citation style.

A discussion of the organization of content for informational reports follows later in this document.

## News Releases

From time to time, the public-service employees may be called upon to prepare a news release for his agency. Whenever the activities of the agency are newsworthy or of interest to the public, the agency has an obligation to report such activities to the press. The most common means for such reporting is by using the press release. Most newspapers and broadcasting stations are initially informed of agencies' activities by news releases distributed by the agencies themselves. Thus, the news release is a basic tool for communicating with the public served by the agency.

The news release is written in news style, with these basic characteristics:

- Sentences are short and simple.

- Paragraphs are short (one or two sentences) and relate to a single item of information.

- Paragraphs are arranged in *inverted order*—the most important in information appears first.

- The first or *lead* paragraph summarizes the entire story. If the reader went no further, he would have the essential information.

- Subsequent paragraphs provide further details, the most important occurring first.

- Reported information is attributed to sources; that is, the source of the news is reported in the story.

- The expression of the writer's opinions is scrupulously avoided.

- The 5 W's (who, what, why, where, when) are included.

News releases should be typed double spaced on standard 8 1/2 x 11 paper, with generous margins and at least 2" of open space above the lead paragraph. Do not write headlines - that is the editor's job. At the top of the first page of the release include the name of the agency releasing the story and the name and phone number of the person to contact if more information is needed. If the release runs more than one page, end each page with the word "-more-" to indicate that more copy follows. End the release with the symbols "###" to indicate that the copy ends at that point.

Accuracy and physical appearance are essential characteristics of the news release. Typographical errors, or errors of fact, such as misspelled names, lead editors to doubt the reliability of the story. Great care should be taken to assure the accuracy and reliability of a news release.

2. REPORTING ON A TOPIC

At one time or another, most public-service employees will be asked to prepare a report on some topic. Usually the need for the report grows out of some policy decision contemplated by the agency for which full information must be considered. For example:

- Should the agency undertake some new project or service?
- Should working conditions be changed?
- Are new specialists needed on the staff?
- Or should a branch office be opened up?

Or any of a hundred other such decisions which the agency must make from time to time.

When called upon to prepare such a report, the employee should have a model to follow which will guide his collection of information and will help him to prepare an effective and useful report.

As with other forms of written communication, both the physical appearance and content of the report are important to create a favorable impression and to engender confidence. The physical appearance of such reports has been discussed earlier; additional suggestions for reports are given in Unit 3. Basic guidelines follow below for organizing and preparing the content.

Preparation for the Report

*What is the Purpose of the Report?* The preparer of the report should have clearly in mind why the report is needed:

- What is the decision being contemplated by the agency?
- To what use will the report be put?

Before beginning to prepare the report, the writer should discuss its purpose fully with the decision-making staff to articulate the purpose the report is intended to serve. If the employee is himself initiating the report, it would be well to discuss its purpose with colleagues to assure that its purpose is clear in his own mind.

*What Questions Should the Report Answer?* Once the purpose of the report is clear, the questions the report must answer may begin to become clear. For example, if the decision faced by the agency is whether or not to offer a new service, questions may be asked such as these:

- What persons would be served by the new service?

- What would the new service cost?
- What new staff would be needed?
- What new equipment and facilities would be needed?
- What alternative ways exist for offering the service?
- How might the new service be administered?

And so on. Unless the purpose of the report is clear, it is difficult to decide what specific questions need to be answered. Once the purpose is clear, these questions can be specified.

*Where Can the Relevant Information be Obtained?* Once the questions are clear in the writer's mind, he can identify the information he will need to answer them. Information may usually be obtained from two general sources:

- *Relevant documents.* Records, publications, and other reports are often useful in locating the information needed to answer particular questions. These may be in the files of the writer's own agency, in other agencies, or in libraries.

- *Personal contacts.* Persons in a position to know the needed information may be contacted in person, by phone, or by letter. Such contacts are especially important in obtaining firsthand accounts of previous experience.

The Text of the Report

*What are the Answers to the Questions?* Once the relevant in-formation is in hand, the answers to the questions may be assembled.

- What does the information reveal? This activity amounts to summarizing the information obtained. It often helps to organize this summary around the specific questions asked by the report. For example, if the report asks in one part, "What are the costs of the new service likely to be?" one section of the report should summarize the information gathered to answer this question.

*Organizing the Report.* The organization of a report into main and subsections depends upon the nature of the report. Reports will differ widely in their organization and treatment. In general, however, the report should generally follow the pattern previously discussed. That is, reports which generally include the following subjects in order will be found to be clear in their intent and to communicate effectively:

- *Description of problem or purpose.* Example: "One problem facing our agency is whether or not we should extend our hours of operation to better serve the public. This report is intended to examine the problem and make recommendations."

- *Questions to be answered.* Example: "In examining this problem, answers were sought to the following questions: What persons would be served? What would it cost? What staff would be needed?"

- *Information sources.* Example: "To answer these questions, letters of complaint for the past three years were examined. Interviews with clients were conducted by phone and in person, phone interviews were conducted with the agency directors in Memphis, Philadelphia, and Chicago."

- *Summary of findings.* Example: "At least 25 percent of the agency's clients would be served better by evening or Saturday service. The costs of operating eight hours of extended service would be negligible, since the service could be provided by rescheduling work assignments. The present staff report they would be inconvenienced by evening and Saturday work assignments."

<u>The Writer's Responsibilities.</u> It is the writer's responsibility to address finally the original purpose of the report. Once the questions have been answered, an informed judgment can be made as to the decision facing the agency. It is at this stage that the writer attempts to draw conclusions from the information he has gathered and summarized. For example, if the original purpose of the report was to help make a decision about whether or not the agency should offer a new service, the writer should draw conclusions from the information and recommend either for or against the new service.

<u>Conclusions and Recommendations.</u> Example: "It appears that operating during extended hours would better serve a significant number of clients. The writer recommends that the agency offer this new service. The present staff should be given temporary assignments to cover the extended hours. As new staff are hired to replace separating persons, they should be hired specifically to cover the extended hours."

3. PERSUASIVE WRITING

Often in life, people are called upon to persuade individuals and groups to adopt ideas believed to be good, or attitudes favorable to ideas thought to be worthwhile or behavior believed to be beneficial. The public service employee may find he must persuade the staff of his own agency, his superiors, the clients of the agency, or the general public in his community.

Persuading others by means of written and other forms of communication is a difficult task and requires much practice. Some principles have emerged from the study of persuasion which may provide some guidelines for developing a model for persuasive writing.

## General Guidelines for Writing Persuasively

*Know the Credibility of the Source.* People are more likely to be persuaded by a message they perceive originates from a trustworthy source. Their trust is enhanced if the source is seen as authoritative, or knowledgeable on the issue discussed in the message. Their trust is increased also if the source appears to have nothing to gain either way, has no vested interest in the final decision. Then, the assertions made in persuasive writing should be backed up by referencing trustworthy and disinterested information sources.

*Avoid Overemotional Appeals.* Appealing to the common emotions of man—love, hate, tear, sex, etc.—can have a favorable effect on the outcome of a persuasive message. But care should be taken because, if the appeal is too strong, it can lead to a reverse effect. For example, if an agency wanted to persuade the public to get chest X-rays, it would have much greater chance of success if it adopted a positive and helpful attitude rather than trying to frighten them into this action. For instance, appealing mildly to the sense of well-being which accompanies knowledge of one's own good health, instead of shocking the public by showing horror pictures of patients who died from lack of timely X-rays.

*Consider the Other Man's Point of View.* To persuade another to one's own point of view, should the writer include information and arguments contrary to his own position? Or should he argue only for his own side?

Generally, it depends on where most of the audience stand in the first place. If most of the audience already favor the position being advocated, then the writer will probably do better including only information favorable to his position. However, if the greater part of the audience are likely to oppose this position, then the writer would probably be better off including their arguments also. In this case, he may be helping his cause by rebutting the opposing arguments as he introduces them into the writing.

An example of this technique might occur in arguing for such an idea as a four-day, forty-hour workweek. Thus: "Many people feel that the ten-hour day is too long and that they would arrive home too late for their regular dinner hour. But think! If you have dinner a littler later each night, you'll have a three-day weekend every week. More days free to go fishing, or camping. More days with your wife and children." That is good persuasive writing!

## Interpersonal Communications

The important role of interpersonal communication in persuading others—face-to-face and person-to-person communications—has been well documented. Mass mailings or printed messages will likely have less effect than personal letters and conversations between persons already known to each other. In any persuasion campaign the personal touch is very important.

An individual in persuading a large number of persons will likely be more effective if he can organize a letter-writing campaign of persuasive messages written by persons favorable to his position to their friends and acquaintances, than if his campaign is based upon sending out a mass mailing of a printed message.

*Conditions for Persuading.* In order for an audience of one or many to be persuaded in the manner desired, these conditions must be met:

- the audience must be *exposed* to the message,
- members of the audience must *perceive* the intent of the message,
- they must *remember* the message afterwards,
- each member must *decide* whether or not to adopt the ideas.

Each member of the audience will respond to a message differently. While every person may receive the message, not everyone will read it. Even among those who read it, not everyone will perceive it in the same way. Some will remember it longer than others. Not everyone will decide to adopt the ideas. These effects are called *selective exposure, selective perception, selective retention,* and *selective decision.*

*The Persuasion Campaign.* How can one counteract these selective effects in persuading others? One thing that is known is that *people tend to be influenced by persuasive messages which they are already predisposed to accept.* This means a person is more likely to persuade people a little than to persuade them a lot.

In planning a persuasion campaign, therefore, the messages should be tailored to the audiences. Success will be more likely if one starts with people who believe *almost* as the writer wants to persuade them to believe—people who are most likely to agree with the position advocated.

The writer also wants to use arguments based on values the particular audience already accepts. For example, in advocating a new teen-age job program, he might argue with business men that the program will help business; with parents, that it will build character; with teachers, that it is educational; with taxpayers, that it will reduce future taxes; and so on.

*The idea is to find some way to make sure that each member of the particular audiences reached can see an advantage for himself, and for the writer to then tailor the messages for those audiences.*

4. INSTRUCTIONAL WRITING

Another task that the public-service employee may expect to face from time to time is the instruction of some other person in the performance of a task. This may sometimes involve preparing written instructions to other employees in the unit, or preparing a training manual for new employees.

It may sometimes involve preparing instructional manuals for clients of the unit, such as "How to Apply for a Real Estate License," "How to Bathe your Baby," or "How to Recognize the Symptoms of Heart Disease."

Whatever the purpose or the audience, certain principles of instruction may be applied which will help make more effective these instructional or training communications. These are: *advance organizers, practice, errorless learning,* and *feedback*.

### Advance Organizers

At or near the beginning of an instructional communication, it helps the learner if he is provided with what can be called an "advance organizer." This element of the communication performs two functions:

- it provides a framework or "map" for the leader to organize the information he will encounter,
- it helps the learner perceive his purpose in learning the tasks which will follow.

The first paragraphs in this section, for example, serve together as an advance organizer. The trainee is informed that he may be called upon to perform these tasks in his job *(perceived purpose),* and that he will be instructed in advance organizers, practice, errorless learning, and feedback *(framework, or "map")*.

### Practice

The notion of *practice makes perfect* is a sound instructional principle. When trying to teach someone to perform a task by means of written communication, the writer should build in many opportunities for practicing the task, or parts of it. This built-in practice should be both appropriate and active:

- *Appropriate practice* is practice which is directly related to learning the tasks at hand.

- *Active practice* is practice in actually performing the task at hand or parts of it, rather than simply reading about the task, or thinking about it.

By inserting questions into the text of the communication, by giving practice quizzes, exercises, or field work, one can build into his instructional communication the kind of practice necessary for the reader to readily learn the task.

## Errorless Learning

The practice given learners should be easy to do. That is, they should not be asked to practice a task if they are likely to make a lot of mistakes. When a mistake is practiced it is likely to recur again and again, like spelling "demons," which have been spelled wrong so often it's difficult to recall the way they should be spelled. Because it is better to practice a task right from the first, it is important that learners do not make errors in practice.

- One method for encouraging correct practice is to give the reader hints, or *prompts,* to help him practice correctly.

- Another method is to instruct him in a logical sequence a little bit at a time. Don't try to teach everything at once. Break the task down into small parts and teach each part of the task in order. Then give the learner practice in each part of the task before giving him practice in the whole thing.

- A third way of encouraging errorless learning is to build in practice and review throughout the communication. The learner may forget part of the task if the teacher doesn't review it with him from time to time.

Remember, people primarily learn from what they do, so build in to the instructional communication many opportunities for the learner to practice correctly all of the parts of the task required for learning, first separately and then all together.

## Feedback

The reader, or learner, can't judge how well he is learning the task unless he is informed of it. In a classroom situation, the teacher usually confirms that the learner has been successful, or points out the errors he made, and provides additional instruction. An instructional communication can also help learners in the same way, by providing *feedback* to the learner.

Following practice, the writer should include in his instructional communication information which will let the reader know whether he performed the task correctly. In case he didn't, the writer should also include some further information which will help the reader perform it correctly next time. This feedback, then, performs two functions:

- it helps the learner confirm that his practice was done correctly, and

- it helps him correct his performance of the task in case he made any errors.

Feedback will be most helpful to the learner if it occurs immediately following practice. The learner should be brought to know of his success or his errors just as soon as possible after practice.

**STUDENT LEARNING ACTIVITIES**

- Write "asking" and "answering" letters, and answer a letter of complaint, using the format assigned by the teacher.

- Write memoranda to other "offices" in a fictitious organization. Plan a field trip using only memos to communicate with other students in the class.

- Take minutes of a small group meeting. Or attend a meeting of the school board and take minutes.

- Write a short report on a public service occupation of special interest to you.

- Write a 15-word telegram reserving a single room at a hotel and asking to be picked up at the airport.

- Write a news release announcing a new service offered to the public by your agency.

- Based upon hearing a reading or pretaping of a report, summarize the report in news style.

- View films on effective communication, for example, *Getting the Facts, Words that Don't Inform,* and *A Message to No One.*

- For a given problem or purpose, compile a list of specific questions you would need to answer to write a report on the topic.

- For a given list of questions, discuss and compile a list of information sources relevant to the questions.

- As a member of a group, consider the problem of "What field trip should the class take to help students learn how to write an effective news release?" What questions will you need to answer? Where will you obtain your information?

- As a member of a group, gather the information and prepare a short report based on it for presentation to the class.

- Write a report on a problem assigned by your teacher.

- Write a brief persuasive letter to a friend on a given topic. Assume he does not already agree with you. Apply principles of source credibility, emotional appeals, and one or both sides of the issue to persuade him.

- Plan a persuasive campaign to persuade a given segment of your community to take some given action.

- Write a short instructional communication on a verbal learning task assigned by your teacher.

- Write a short instructional communication on a learning task which involves the operation of equipment.

- Try your instructional communications with a fellow student to check for errors during practice.

**TEACHER MANAGEMENT ACTIVITIES**

- Have students practice letter writing. Assign letters of "asking" and "answering." Read them a letter of complaint and ask them to write an answering letter. Establish common rules of format and style for each assignment. Change the rules from time to time to give practice in several styles.

- Have small groups plan an event, such as a field trip, assigning the various tasks to one another using only memoranda. Evaluate the effectiveness of each group's memo writing by the speed and completeness of their planning.

- Have the class attend a public meeting. Assign each the task of taking the minutes. Evaluate the minutes for brevity and completeness.

- Encourage each student to prepare a short report on a public service occupation of special interest to himself.

- Give the students practice in writing 15-word telegrams.

- Have the students prepare a news release announcing some new service offered to the public, such as "Taxpayers can now obtain help from the Internal Revenue Service in completing their income tax forms as a result of a new service now being offered by the agency."

- Give the students practice in summarizing and writing leads by giving them the facts of a news event and asking them to write a one or two-sentence lead summarizing the significant facts of the event.

- Read a speech or a story. Have students write a summary and a report of the speech or story in news style.

- Show films on effective communication, for example, *Getting the Facts, Words that Don't Inform,* and *A Message to No One.*

- State a general problem and have each student prepare a list of the specific questions implied by the problem.

- State a list of specific questions and discuss with the class the sources of information which might bear upon each of the questions.

- Have small groups consider and write short reports jointly on the general problem, "What field trip should the class take to help students learn how to write an effective news release?" Have each group identify the specific questions to be answered, with sources for needed information.

- Have each student identify and prepare a short report on a general problem of interest.

- Assign students to work in groups of three or four to draft a letter to a friend to persuade him to make a contribution to establish a new city art museum.

- Assign the students to groups of five or six, each group to map out a persuasive campaign on a given topic. Some topics are "Give Blood," "Get Chest X-Ray," "Quit Smoking," "Don't Litter," "Inspect Your House Wiring," etc.

- Have each student identify a simple verbal learning task and prepare an instructional communication to teach that task to another student not familiar with the task.

- Have each student prepare an instructional manual designed to train someone to operate some simple piece of equipment, such as an adding machine, a slide projector, a tape recorder, or something of similar complexity.

- Have each student try his instructional communication out on another student, unfamiliar with the task. He should observe the activities and responses of the trial student to identify errors made in practice. He should revise the communication, adding practice, review, and prompts wherever needed to reduce errors in practice.

# EVALUATION QUESTIONS

### Written Communications

1. Which type of letter would be correct for a public service worker to send?   1.____

    A. A letter containing erasures
    B. A letter reflecting goodwill
    C. A rude letter
    D. An impersonal letter

2. Memos usually leave out:   2.____

    A. Complimentary closings
    B. The name of the sender
    C. The name of the addressee
    D. The date the memo was sent

3. A good business letter would not contain:   3.____

    A. Short, simple words, sentences, and paragraphs
    B. Information contained in the letter being answered
    C. Concrete nouns and active verbs
    D. Orderly placed paragraphs

4. In writing business letters it is important to:   4.____

    A. Use a conversational tone
    B. Use a hard, cold tone
    C. Use abstract words
    D. Use a passive tone

5. Messages between departments in an agency are usually sent by:   5.____

    A. Letter
    B. Memo
    C. Telegram
    D. Long reports

6. Repetitive work can be simplified by the use of:   6.____

    A. Memos
    B. Telegrams
    C. Forms
    D. Reports

7. In filling out forms and applications, it is important to be:   7.____

    A. Legible
    B. Complete
    C. Accurate
    D. All of the above

8. Memos should be:

   A. Clear
   B. Brief
   C. Complete
   D. All of the above

9. Minutes of meetings should not include:

   A. The opinions of the recorder
   B. The approval of previous minutes
   C. The corrections of previous minutes
   D. The voting members present

10. Reports are written by public service workers to:

    A. Assemble information in one place
    B. Aid the organization in making decisions
    C. Inform the public and other agencies
    D. All of the above

11. News releases should include:

    A. A lead paragraph summarizing the story
    B. Long paragraphs about many topics
    C. The writer's opinion
    D. All of the above

12. Readers of news releases and reports are influenced by the:

    A. Content of the material
    B. Accuracy of the material
    C. Physical appearance of the material
    D. All of the above

13. The contents of a report should include:

    A. A description of the problem
    B. The questions to be answered
    C. Unimportant information
    D. A summary of findings

14. People tend to be influenced easier if:

    A. They can see something in the position that would be advantageous to them
    B. They are almost ready to agree anyhow
    C. The appeal to the emotions is not overly strong
    D. All of the above

## KEY (CORRECT ANSWERS)

1. B
2. A
3. B
4. A
5. B

6. C
7. D
8. D
9. A
10. D

11. A
12. D
13. C
14. D

www.ingramcontent.com/pod-product-compliance
Lightning Source LLC
Chambersburg PA
CBHW082045300426
44117CB00015B/2619